840.7
Jon

157427

Jones.
The assault on French literature.

**Learning Resources Center
Nazareth College of Rochester, N. Y.**

*THE ASSAULT
ON
FRENCH LITERATURE
AND OTHER ESSAYS*

The Assault on French Literature

AND OTHER ESSAYS

by

P. MANSELL JONES

Emeritus Professor of Modern French Literature in the University of Manchester

GREENWOOD PRESS, PUBLISHERS
WESTPORT, CONNECTICUT

Library of Congress Cataloging in Publication Data

Jones, Percy Mansell.
  The assault on French literature, and other essays.

  Reprint of the ed. published by Manchester University Press, Manchester, Eng.
  Includes bibliographical references.
  CONTENTS: The recovery of French studies.--French before sunrise.--The assault on French literature. [etc.]
   1. French literature--Study and teaching. 2. French literature--History and criticism--Addresses, essays, lectures. I. Title.
  [PQ45.J6 1976]   840'.7   75-26214
  ISBN 0-8371-8401-0

© 1963 P. Mansell Jones

Originally published in 1963 by Manchester University Press, Manchester, Eng.

Reprinted with the permission of Manchester University Press

Reprinted in 1976 by Greenwood Press, a division of Williamhouse-Regency Inc.

Library of Congress Catalog Card Number 75-26214

ISBN 0-8371-8401-0

Printed in the United States of America

TO
EUGÈNE VINAVER

'Mais oui, Monsieur, de tout mon cœur et au nom de tous nos confrères, je peux et j'aime vous confier que notre fierté d'accueillir en vous un maître et un érudit se double de la joie de saluer en lui le meilleur et le plus averti des amateurs de poèmes.'

—*From M. Maurice Delbouille's speech for the reception of Professor Vinaver at the Académie Royale of Belgium on the sixteenth of December, 1961.*

CONTENTS

		Page
PREFACE		ix

PART ONE
BASIC ISSUES

I	THE RECOVERY OF FRENCH STUDIES	3
II	FRENCH BEFORE SUNRISE	8
III	THE ASSAULT ON FRENCH LITERATURE	27
IV	MODERN HUMANITIES IN THE TECHNOLOGICAL AGE	60
V	PROFICIENCY IN MODERN LANGUAGES	77

PART TWO
COMMENTARIES & DISCUSSIONS

VI	THE FORMAL METHOD ARRAIGNED	89
VII	THE ENGLISH APPROACH TO RONSARD	105
VIII	BAUDELAIRE'S POEM, *Le Cygne*	121
IX	LAFORGUE'S *vers libre* AND THE FORM OF *The Waste Land*	133
X	VERLAINE AND RIMBAUD	146
XI	INTRODUCING *Du Côté de chez Swann*	161
XII	ANDRÉ GIDE: ANGLES OF APPROACH	176
	APPENDIX A Review of R. M. Albérès: *L'Aventure intellectuelle du XXe siècle*	190

PREFACE

IN this book I offer some critical observations and constructive suggestions on the presentation of what is still, for the majority of us in Britain, the most attractive of foreign literatures. The title chosen for the collection would lose little of its significance, at least for the author, if limitations of headline space allowed him to use a rubric of this kind: 'Thoughts on the making of a modern discipline with examples and reservations drawn from the régime and practices of previous decades.' My descriptions and disclosures of what went wrong in the past will have, it is hoped, an encouraging effect. They demonstrate by contrast what improvements in the organization of studies have been made, especially during the years of expansion so well turned to account since the last world war.

Of the many grounds for rejoicing that one recognizes in the present phase of educational discussion, none is more reassuring than the willingness of the authorities to accept the principle of change and adaptation rather than to resist all initiative with the obduracy or evasiveness practised in some quarters even as recently as thirty years ago. Yet when one thinks of the condition of humane studies and the risk they run of being degraded to the status of poor relations of the sciences, a source of disquietude persists. What improvements have occurred in them seem to have been due less to intrinsic developments within the disciplines themselves than to the results of changes happening in the world outside, vibrations from which impinge on the curriculum through impersonal channels, altering its contents, as it were, *par la force des choses*. A radical weakness that has afflicted most of the educational efforts of our time—at least until staff-student (or -pupil) ratios were improved—is the inertia or complacency that could wait for wars and revolutions to precipitate reforms that were obviously long in arrears.

It took the first world war to shake modern studies out of the sloth I describe in Chapter II. Today, 'the spirit of interest in modern languages which', it is predicted,[1] 'will doubtless soon swell with a cataract of words followed, it is to be hoped, by action', has been brought about, not by any autonomous movement of internal revision or adjustment but, explicitly, in consequence of 'the Government's decision to negotiate Britain's entry into the Common European Community and the common market'.[2]

It is assumed in the Headmasters' report that the chief aim of teaching and learning languages is to be able to communicate. With this, taken broadly, one may feel in complete agreement. But the presentation of the case would seem to suggest that the main incentive to communication is the promotion of business. 'It is clear', runs a quotation from the report, 'that the place of languages in the curriculum will be revolutionized as we find our daily lives and jobs enmeshed in ever closer collaboration with our European neighbours at all levels of technology, industry and commerce.' As if to confirm these practical incentives, objections are raised to the syllabus prescribed for the A level examination, 'in so far as it encouraged concentration on standard literary classics as the main or only reading matter, and encouraged pupils

---

[1] This phrase comes from an editorial leader on 'Languages' in the *Times Educational Supplement*, 23 March 1962. It comments on the report of a working party set up by the Lancashire and Cheshire Branch of the Incorporated Association of Head Masters.

[2] From 'Languages in the Curriculum', ibid., p. 574.—May the impulse to improve proficiency in languages not be checked by our failure to participate in the E.E.C.

to attempt over-sophisticated, because premature, literary criticism'. To this what are we to say?

With the implied appeal for a more accurate and versatile knowledge of foreign languages I am (though not an example of the good linguist) again in sympathy. Considerable numbers of pupils and students whom I have examined in my time have not known the languages presumed to have been taught them nearly as well as could have been expected, when the length of their initiation (often, in the case of undergraduates, from nine to eleven years) is taken into account. As for the teaching of literature, the chapter I have called 'French before Sunrise' will show some of the follies that have been perpetrated under that head. Yet a protest representing the views of Headmasters which values the commercial use of languages, while it appears to depreciate what could be gained from contact with the classical writers of a great literature, fills one with the kind of apprehension I have tried to analyse in the case of the Positivistic tendencies discussed in Chapter III. How, for instance, is international understanding (accepted as an objective by the sponsors of the report) to be secured through the media of language and literature, if some examples of a nation's written classics are not to be seriously studied by the young aspirants?

Although the chapter on 'Proficiency in Modern Languages' deals mainly with a written test (translation *from* the foreign tongue), I still think that the doubts it expresses exceed the *ad hoc* use of the exercise for examining purposes and are generally valid and justifiable today. It is an unfortunate fact that arguments about proficiency tend to become partial and one-sided. Some teachers plump for the objective of oral fluency at all costs; others esteem a grammatical grounding to be indispensable. What I have always had in mind, or rather, *on* my mind, is concern about *general reading power*. And my concern applies not only to the 'sixth-former' coming up to the University or on the point of leaving school, but even to the majority of Honours candidates who may have given abundant signs of knowing the languages of their prescribed texts, but who, I often suspect, are in reliable and active possession of a vocabulary the limits of which would surprise anyone capable of submitting its extent, variety and precision to a reasonably exacting scrutiny.

To place the joint cause of reading and translation in its broadest perspective, two important considerations should be mentioned, although limits of space will not allow much to be said about either. The first is the increasing demand for professional translators and official interpreters. Despite the prospect of rapid developments in mechanical devices for translating, opportunities for personal expertise seem still to be very promising. Rigorous courses in the training of translators are available abroad, specifically in Geneva and Paris. But signs are few that much has been done in this country to prepare for such openings.[1]

The second consideration prompted by the demands of the moment is one I had the occasion to present recently before an audience of scholars and teachers. To stress the importance of reading presupposes a provision of books worthy to be read. This involves critical choice but also literal expense. I therefore make an appeal for an increase in permanent lending stocks designed for the joint use of modern language teachers and the general reader. To establish collections of sufficient scope and variety financial support would have to be found outside the profession; and the management of the stocks would presumably have to be entrusted to the staffs of the municipal and county libraries. Teachers at work in big towns can usually find in the local

[1] See Eva Paneth, 'The Interpreter's Task and Training', *Universities Quarterly*, November 1958.

libraries selections varying from a few dozens to five or ten times that number. The Chief Librarian of Manchester City informed me, a few years ago, that there were over 15,000 books printed in foreign languages on the shelves in his charge. But the range of their effective use could hardly have extended beyond the city boundaries. The result is that very many language teachers in posts throughout the provinces stand the risk of being bibliographically starved.

The moral is obvious. There sits the undergraduate in the library of his university or of his department, surrounded by more books of interest to him than he would care to count. A year or two later, appointed, shall we say? to carry the clear light of French reason into darkest England or Wales, he may not have a book on his subject to lay hands on, except those he has brought with him or the texts prescribed for the year's work. School libraries are still too irregularly stocked to constitute a reliable category. And book prices have soared by as much abroad as they have done at home.

The question of public costs, I repeat, need not be raised. What we should raise are our voices. A nation that can, even in a year of drastic restrictions, devote fifty million pounds to running its universities—nearly three-quarters of which amount goes to the sciences and most of that to technology—should be able to spare the comparatively trifling sums that would help to promote the culture of languages, even after the library grant has been raised from the feeble 3·8 per cent to the fabulous 3·9.

The cultivation of the native language in France through consistent teaching from the primary school to the *lycée* has stirred the admiration and the envy of intelligent people in most other countries. The study of the national literature has also, for about half a century, received serious pedagogical attention. This, however, has proceeded from centres of systematic initiative capable of exerting official pressure with results that have tended to harden into a stereotyped routine.

With the rigours and limitations of method deplored by a *professeur de lycée* from whose protest I quote in Chapter VI, it would be interesting to contrast the situation in our country. Here during the last thirty years the presentation of literature in universities and schools has been transformed by new modes of approach, analysis and appraisal that have drawn their inspiration from the free critical study of texts, and have in turn helped to revivify the practice of literary criticism.

Whereas in France during the same period the alienation of academic studies from the contemporary movements in criticism seems to have been almost complete. How many French students since the first world war have not shared the feelings of the critic and novelist, Marcel Arland, of whom it was recently said: 'Marcel Arland déplore l'indifférence des professeurs à ce que la jeunesse ardente d'après-guerre, en quête de richesses intérieures et de valeurs spirituelles, pouvait attendre de la littérature, réduite chez eux, lui semblait-il, à l'état de sciences'?

There can be little doubt that the prime mover in broadening the divergence between scholarship and criticism was an energetic historian of literature whose authority and example were dominant in France during the early decades of this century and whose widespread influence is perceptible even today. Most recent manuals still find a place for Gustave Lanson; but it is usually restricted to a paragraph as in the standard edition of Bédier et Hazard. The indefatigable scholar is praised for two things: his own *Histoire de la Littérature française*, first published in 1894, and the bibliographical manuals which were his main preoccupation during the early decades of this century. If in our contemporary histories we compare the place given to Lanson with that devoted to Hippolyte Taine, whose 'system' Lanson constantly attacked, the contrast is striking. Taine receives twenty times the space allotted to his critic because, of course, Taine's system was a hypothesis which he could treat lightly: Lanson's system was his 'method' which, once forged, he could not escape.

Even today his History attracts, and deserves to attract, many admirers. But it is odd to find so astute and dissatisfied a critic as Etiemble commending its author for a phrase in the preface, without admitting that the advice Lanson gave in 1894[1] represented an attitude to literary studies which his later thought and productions—abetted by his strenuous propaganda for 'scientific' history—ignored and tacitly discredited, not without equivocations which suggest that the dogmatic theorist felt less sure of himself than he sounded.

Were it not for the protest wrung from the heart of the *professeur de lycée* whom I have mentioned, I should have been tempted to assume that Gustave Lanson's example and doctrine had exerted a less persistent effect on the presentation of French literature in France than abroad. There can, however, be no doubt that his influence and that of his disciples has been extensive and durable. The strength of his effort was to base literary scholarship on fact rather than on impression. The weakness of his doctrine was to identify this effort with the presentation of literature. The error was shared by his disciples who succumbed, as he did, to the wave of scientific positivism that invaded the Faculté des Lettres, mainly at Lanson's bidding, during and after his tenure of the Chair of Eloquence at the Sorbonne.

General support for these contentions has been brought to my notice in an important pronouncement made by the late

[1] See Chapter III, pp. 29–31.

Professor Leo Spitzer shortly before he died.[1] Professor Spitzer did not criticize the Lansonians, but he lamented the curb upon stylistic studies exerted by the positivistic cast and background of French literary scholarship.

'Une autre raison de la carence stylistique', he said, 'est l'esprit général des études littéraires en France, qui malgré la variété des tempéraments, restent encore imprégnées du positivisme scientifique du XIXe siècle, ou plutôt de la tendance à découvrir l'enchaînement de "causes" qui expliqueraient l'œuvre littéraire—au lieu, comme le conseillait Montaigne, de "laisser là les causes" et de s'occuper plutôt des "choses", c'est-à-dire, dans notre cas, de la description des œuvres littéraires. Si le désir de rivaliser en exactitude avec les sciences naturelles justifie jusqu'à un certain degré le scientisme du XIXe siècle en matière littéraire, telle n'est plus la situation au XXe, qui a vu s'affaiblir les explications causales même dans les sciences naturelles. La grande peur des humanistes français, c'est encore aujourd'hui celle de ne pas être aussi scientifiques que les scientifiques. . . .'

Another reason for the decay of stylistic analysis in France was found by Professor Spitzer in the existence of what he called 'la pratique scolaire de l'*explication de textes*', the development of which to a certain level prevents, he thought, the rise of a similar technique to a higher level still.

Here, in this epitome of a judgement external and superior to my own, I find the main themes I have been trying for some years to disengage and develop in the theoretical discussions now collected in this book. I hope it will not seem pretentious if, taking my chapter on the 'Assault' at last off

[1] I have to thank Professor Vinaver for directing my attention to the speech Professor Spitzer made at the eighth Congress of the Fédération Internationale des Langues et Littératures modernes, held at Liège in 1960. See *Les Etudes de Style et les Différents Pays*, collected in the Bibliothèque de la Faculté de Philosophie et Lettres de l'Université de Liège. Fascicule CLXI, 1961.

the stocks, I offer it either as a premeditation on, or as an amplification of, the thoughts expressed by the Master who spoke with such pungency and authority at Liège.

The pieces in 'Commentaries and Discussions' are, with one exception, exercises in how to introduce literary topics within the official lecture 'hour' of fifty minutes. Hence their discursive manner and conversational tone. They were delivered on the invitation of Heads of departments at university or institutional centres in various parts of Britain and are reproduced with their permission and encouragement. Most of them have been prepared for publication under the direction of Mrs J. M. Sutcliffe, Assistant Secretary of the Manchester University Press. I wish to thank her for expert and patient advice on the presentation of this book. To my friend, Mr J. H. Watkins, Senior Lecturer, University College, Bangor, I owe special acknowledgements for exact and generous help with the correction of proofs. His wise suggestions for improving the text of this collection have been gratefully adopted.

P. M. J.

December 1962

PART ONE
BASIC ISSUES

I

THE RECOVERY OF FRENCH STUDIES[1]

IT is a strange experience, impressive yet amusing, to look back, from this point of vantage, along the road traversed in so arduous a pilgrimage as mine has been. Impressive because of the many privileges I have received; amusing because of the way things began.

My first lessons in French could only provoke your indulgent smiles to hear about. They were the intimations gathered in childhood from unpretentious relatives about the French, their ways and their works. Slight as they were I often think that those early impressions were far more attractive, more real and more true to the spirit of France than what is often experienced by youngsters today, who get their first knowledge of things French from a chart of the larynx on a classroom wall with a few phonetic signs in the margin, or from the disquieting appearance of the parts of an irregular verb in a grammar book.

My initiation was haphazard but more alluring. France to the people with whom I was brought up was a country of refinement and audacity—though they wouldn't have used abstractions to describe it. To them it was essentially a land of fine workmanship, as exhibited in articles of attire from

[1] From a reply to the presentation of a volume of *Studies in Modern French Literature* (Manchester University Press) which took place in the University of Manchester on 16 March 1961. Reprinted from the *Manchester University Gazette*, June 1961.

gloves, silks and other fabrics, to the latest fashions and styles in shoes, hats and coiffures. But France was also noted amongst us for the arts of life: polite manners, graceful gestures, sparkling talk. And, of course, for the fine arts: pictures, prints, drawings and reproductions usually in sepia of vast Gothic naves and chancels dimly lit from stained-glass windows, with gargoyles and hobgoblins lurking around.

My father, a small businessman, had (luckily for me) escaped a systematic education, and so had found time and energy to pick up all sorts of things fresh for himself. Just for the fun of it, he had pasted into a home-made album some excellent photographs, including a few of great French figures and paintings and churches. From them came hints of the splendours of French history—what you would call the national *panache*. And such impressions were reinforced by gifts from an uncle who liked to go on a jaunt to Paris and pretend he had witnessed the glories of the Second Empire. To keep up the delusion he would send us old copies of illustrated papers, heavily bound and full of sketches of French life and manners under Napoleon III. There they were: vicious but attractive-looking dandies, so unlike our good Mr Gladstone, and whose sartorial finish put even Mr Disraeli in the shade; ladies too with very low necks and no sleeves to their gowns—so unlike our good Queen Victoria and her Maids of Honour . . . but good for a change, my father would say. And abundant vignettes of French army officers in képis with scarlet-striped, long baggy trousers and dainty box-calf boots, their sabres shimmering and their spurs twinkling like stars at their heels. All very elegant with a touch of languor—but you should see them in the attack! My father had been christened Arnaud after the Chevalier de Saint-Arnaud of Crimean fame, and he was impressed by what he had read of *la fureur française*. True, the

Imperial Guard had been licked at Waterloo; but that was a long time ago; and France always rose to her feet, unfurled the *gonfalon*, blew the *oliphant*, soared aloft like the phoenix and was soon as full of dash and as smart as ever.

Such were the notes struck for the *fleur de lys* in the years before the locusts had eaten the bloom away.

The dream of Chivalry didn't survive my first week in a French Department. The grand old *Chanson de Roland*, which my poor father's hints and tips had prepared me to enjoy, was deviscerated: the locusts ate the glamour and spirit right out of it, leaving a litter of broken words. But the song still sang a heroic *laisse* or two in our second-hand copies of Léon Gautier's edition. Secretly, surreptitiously, you could even *read* the text by candlelight in your modest 'digs'—away from the shadow of Professor Tausendteufel and his bag of lethal instruments.

If the laborious studies of my distant youth—based alas! on as good a set of texts as the Middle Ages could produce—turned out to be a grubbing exercise in verbal roots, I must confess that my own early teaching suffered from much the same vice in another form: too rigorous an addiction to *les exigences de la méthode*. It was not a presentation of texts as literature but a premature imposition of 'influence' technique foisted upon tyros in literary history, before either they or their teacher had read a hundredth part of the books whose titles adorned the continuous spate of notes. You may well ask: 'Why did you do so much of it?' Because everyone was doing it, trapped in a vicious circle. The subject was defined as the History of French Literature and was examined as defined; and therefore had to be taught as it was examined....

But I speak of a past that had better be forgotten. What a relief to have received, before reaching the end of my tether, an invitation to join a school of French studies, where none of these black arts was practised! One had moved into a milieu, and indeed into a period, characterized everywhere by experiment and freedom. Enlightened guidance had gone far to efface the errors of the earlier decades; and the post-war recruits to the profession were, and are, men and women of so much ability and devotion that it is feared their like will not be found again in nearly sufficient numbers to cope with the problems and products of 'expansion'. The concept of humane studies in our time has become clearer—if it is not yet as clear as some of us could wish—and a renewed sense of responsibility, not only for the advancement of knowledge, but for the quality of culture, is rapidly gaining ground. The importance of preparing leaders for the next generation is recognized—leaders not only in academic prowess but, to borrow words Earl Russell used recently of a great scholar, leaders in 'salvaging civilization'. Such a task is not likely to be finished in a decade. The fight for civilization is one of those wars from which there is no discharge. If I may risk another lofty image, while the life of the spirit breathes on the troubled waters of our time, changes must occur in ever more rapid succession, and they are all likely to be charged from the same dynamos of scientific power, with danger or with hope. But now more than ever the choice between destruction and utopia seems to rest, not with the discoverers or with the inventors, but with the educators. Among the shrinking proportion of humanists, special incentives await the sponsors of the younger disciplines—these mobile, malleable, upstart modern humanities with their multiple facets and their immense potential. This field we must explore in good heart, not merely in a spirit of anxious concern, but for the vista of exhilarating opportunities it has to offer.

Otherwise in the transformations that are at hand—the effects of which we have not yet begun to feel—we might find ourselves relegated to a role of mere utility: teaching good pronunciation and the names of the latest novelists to the daughters of the Technocrats, before they flit over to Paris in the family helicopter.

The hegemony of the sciences is for the moment at least an unquestioned fact. But does this not mean that, in the matter of initiatives, we modern linguists may never have had it so good? Many of the strong positions lost at present by the ancient classics are open to be gained by the resurgent spirit of France, the light and vigour of whose intelligent collaboration in salvaging civilization we doubtless wish to help in keeping undimmed and undiminished.

Science, properly understood, gives us each a chance to find his place in the university hierarchy.

Going through a laboratory not long ago, I was shown a receptacle in which powerful agents were juxtaposed awaiting complete fusion. Presently the demonstrator in charge opened the vessel and shook his duster over the aperture. 'Why did you do that?' I asked. 'Ah,' he said, 'that's the secret of the catalyst.'

The allegory is clear. Insignificant intruder into the realm of fine scholarship, the name of Jones impressed on the cover of this handsome volume has sufficed to bring together a learned constellation of the first order.

I have long felt that the only purpose in life to which I might aspire would be to help better men to make better books. That boon has been granted by whatever gods there be, thanks to your generous mediation; and all that I can do in turn is to express bewildered but heartfelt thanks for your gift.

II

FRENCH BEFORE SUNRISE

'Uncontaminated exaltation of uselessness in its most benign form is best studied among teachers of languages.'
—Lancelot Hogben, *Dangerous Thoughts*

THERE is a history of the modern university yet to be written, that of the students who have toiled, suffered, triumphed or succumbed in the conditions it has provided. The commemorative volumes of the newer establishments make consistently cheerful reading, but they leave a great deal out. They tell of the founders and their co-adjutors who laid the bases of construction and finance, inaugurated the departments, contrived the administrative schemes and steered the new ships on all too little fuel through the hazards of their maiden voyages. But how have the undergraduates fared, crowded in their holds, from which when the cruise is over so many have emerged into a world of chance and luck, unsuspected in its dimensions of opportunity and frustration? The full story can never be told until the obscure and complicated history of teaching and learning in arts and science subjects is unravelled from what documentary evidence remains to support the reminiscences of those who can think back to the days of hardship and heroism for the teacher as well as for the student.

Through lack of critical records, apart from examiners' classifications and administrators' statistics, I propose to refer to some of my own experiences in the belief (for which external evidence has accrued) that, allowing for local differences and personal eccentricities, much of what I went through as an undergraduate was in varying degrees characteristic of the experience of great numbers of students in arts, or at least in modern studies, during the decades before the first world war, and of not a few since. If I stress the weaker elements in my university education, while acknowledging that many of its defects have been removed, it is because I think that certain radical errors and inadequacies have persisted from the drafting of curricula and the rough-hewing of methods over half a century ago. Too little is known of the mischief in our roots, our unoriginal sins.

I must be careful to say at the outset that the uningratiating impressions to be described do not, to any comparable degree, represent my experience of university life as a whole. Since graduation my horoscope has revealed itself so rich in favourable aspects that, if I were reproached with ingratitude for attempting to dig up the past, the only excuse I could offer is the conviction that the Alma Mater can be so much more thoughtful on behalf of her graduates than of her undergraduates, whose needs are not all satisfied with places of refreshment, recreation and repose. In my student days the good lady's hands were tied, and before telling my story I must indicate some of the circumstances and conditions that help to extenuate her faults.

Many of the defects that quickly or gradually disclosed themselves in the modern establishments proceeded from deficiencies for which no individual could be blamed. Chief of these was a grievous shortage of funds. The departments were deplorably understaffed. Scanty equipment discouraged experiment and the provision of books could be embarrassingly small. The library of the College I entered was, thanks to generous bequests, by no means so limited in stocks as were many of those in other provincial universities even a few decades later. But long after my undergraduate days the personnel responsible for presenting a subject could be restricted to two or three members. Many of my contemporaries will have known of more than one department run by a single teacher, and may be able to recall the prowess of some of those primeval giants who would lend a hand with the teaching of two or three subjects other than their own. To vociferate for twenty-five hours a week was a task the hardiest of them undertook with equanimity and they were as much beloved for their geniality as admired for their versatility. As an offset to what is to follow, let it here be said that men of fine gifts and abundant good-will could be found in every centre. Without their faith, insight and determination the new foundations could not have survived their early decades of indigence. The modern departments stand as memorials to the devotion of a few rare spirits.

But now let us glance at the curriculum, remembering that very much depends not merely on how a scheme of studies is composed, but on how it is presented. In the early days six and even eight subjects could be prescribed for the first year. By my time the number of Intermediate courses had been reduced to four. Recently they have come down to three. The original intention was no doubt to broaden the basis of the beginner's interests, following what was understood to be the Scots model. The idea was not unreasonable, but it proved impracticable. The need to enlarge the student's horizon was never more generally recognized than it is today when it has become a pressing problem. But no solution could be reached by introducing him to a diversity of skills in a number of different subjects. Such dispersion of efforts usually ended in accumulations of bits and pieces picked up in what are sometimes called 'end-stopped' courses in the rudiments. Since my student days the tendency has been to cut down the miscellany of departmental requirements so as to allow for more active concentration on fewer disciplines carried further. This tendency is, I think, right. Unfortunately, however, the modes of training which it encourages are often too narrow to provide for the adequate education of the undergraduate.

At this point we have to consider the incidence of a new dispersive force, the effects of which threaten the best laid schemes of study with a fragmentation more insidious than all the diversions and distractions of the former multiple arrangement.

Few who have no experience of the state of the universities before the first world war could realize how greatly the impact of research has increased in extent, momentum and influence during the last forty years. Referring to the corresponding change in America, Dr Robert Hutchins says:

No university can now be called respectable that is not respectable in research. Fifty years ago it was just the other way round. Universities were then colleges of liberal arts with professional schools attached. The campaign for research as the distinguishing character of the university was not won until yesterday.[1]

I clearly remember the time when research, the word and the activity, was associated mainly with the operations and the nomenclature of the sciences. Survivors of my period of academic incubation may recall how few university teachers on the arts side made any profession of active scholarship and how many remained all their lives content with nominal degree qualifications. The contempt they would express for the pretensions of novices who, they thought, had not read widely enough to undertake serious investigations on the strength of Honours in a subject, showed no lack of judgement on their part. But the intrepid tyros they disapproved

---

[1] *The University of Utopia.* Cf. 'Research was not yet invented': quoted in Sir Geoffrey Faber's *Jowett*, p. 168. For a brief discussion of the objection felt to using the word 'research' for advanced study in the Humanities see the *Oxford University Handbook*, p. 173.

of could not help noticing that the breadth and power of learning which many of their seniors were presumed to possess appeared to inspire surprisingly few of them to make contributions of any importance to their subjects. It gave us a feeling of unaccustomed assurance to chance upon the name of any of our teachers at the foot of an article. Few of them appeared to realize that the tide had set against them and would soon be effacing the armchair type of scholar like a wrinkle in the sand. Actually the flood of specialization had already gone far to multiply, diversify and confuse the contents of the curriculum. Accepted as inevitable in the sciences, the subdivision of intellectual labour had spread to all subjects. And it is from the ensuing fragmentation of studies that two of our most disturbing educational problems have arisen: that of disrupting the balance of school work through prematurely intensive studies imposed by university entrance requirements and that of side-tracking the undergraduate's attention from the main interest of his subject.

Research, we all know, can improve the presentation of a subject through renewing its conception. What is not so readily admitted is the fact that the influence of research on teaching can—at least in arts subjects—have bad as well as good consequences. The encouragement given to investigation and the fascination with the quest for new knowledge have tended to produce curricula marred by a restless empiricism rather than characterized by a well meditated organization of connected studies centred in the improvement of the student's mind. The unfortunate effects of specialization and the lack of judicious adaptation could hardly be more flagrantly illustrated than by reverting to the earlier forms of some of the most popular courses in arts.

While the sciences were developing more or less harmoniously, owing to the fact that science teaching departments were of relatively recent foundation, far less basic similarity, less unanimity and still less equality of esteem could be found between subjects in the faculty of arts. Some, like Greek and Latin, were heirs to a long tradition of pedagogical experience and remained well adapted to those pupils who came from schools that could provide a good grounding. On the other hand *parvenus* like the modern languages were for long managed with a lack of pedagogical tact that amounted to a caricature of good sense. Few subjects could show more clearly the misapplication of research conceptions and practices to their presentation as disciplines.

The story is often told of how it was decided to present modern languages to undergraduates. For me its significance lies in the revelation of the paucity of thought that went into the foundation of a new kind of subject destined for an important role in the faculty of arts. Napier, the first Merton Professor of English at Oxford (concerning whom Lewis Farnell expressed the doubt as to whether he could appreciate a text as literature) is reported to have said, when asked for an opinion, that, since you could not make a discipline out of a modern literature, you must stiffen the course with linguistics. I have often wondered whether any other explicit reason was given why chairs of French were founded in this country as professorships of Romance Philology. Anyhow by 1920 a Government report complained that 'in attempting too much the reformers did not secure that the languages themselves should be learnt.'[1]

No truer verdict could have been passed on my experience of a modern language department in 1908. The living tongue was not taught at all, except through weekly exercises in written composition on the Latin prose model. An exercise in dictation was occasionally improvised with disastrous results, blazoned by superb slashes of the red pencil. A little

[1] *Modern Studies: Report of the Committee on the Position of Modern Languages.* H.M.S.O. Reprint, 1928. See §§ 6–7.

more regularly we lisped through passages for translation drawn from what seemed to us prodigiously difficult modern French authors with whom we had no chance at all of becoming better acquainted. The passages of English set for *thème* were likewise so picturesque that many of them refused to go into French even when our teacher helped himself out with the aid of a familiar crib. So that, as is the way with that sacrosanct exercise if mismanaged, we were continuously contaminating our exiguous stock of *la belle langue* with our own reiterated errors. The jibe that living languages were taught in university departments as if they were dead languages was in my student days and for long after well earned.

Literature after 1850 had no place in syllabuses published down to at least 1910. The preponderant incidence of the teaching fell on the medieval and renaissance periods with special emphasis on early forms of the language treated etymologically. By an ordinance of sublime egoism the whole of the French Renaissance could be omitted from the Honours course if the student consented to do Provençal with the professor.[1] The grand design of presenting the language and literature of France from the 'earliest monuments' to the mid-nineteenth century collapsed after the year 1600 in an avalanche of débris. From the welter, which included fragments of the greatest of all centuries of French culture, you picked up what you could, if you could pick yourself up. I am afraid I was too dazed to be able to recall anything more, except taking down from dictation the sequence of the plots of Racine's plays. For pious reasons apparently, samples of eighteenth-century literature were excluded from the programme, and as for Romanticism, hadn't we done the lyrical poets in school?

[1] For evidence of this preposterous alternative see the Calendar of the University of Wales for 1907.

Murmurs frequently arose against this odd arrangement of 'modern' studies. Comparisons were drawn between the treatment of British students of French and that of French students who, it was claimed, were not subjected to similar requirements in the study of their own language. As late as the 1940's complaints made by members of the National Union of Students seemed to indicate the persistence of the same bias, at least in some centres. The official defence was dogmatic but vague. The living languages should be learnt abroad. Access to medieval studies was the exclusive gift of a university department. Subsequent phases of literature anyone could study simply by reading (on the strength of a vocabulary whose limits were betrayed in our deplorable dictation exercises!).

Let us look a little more closely into the prescriptions and the way they were applied. What was defined as the 'basic course' for Honours comprised three medieval texts: the *Chanson de Roland*, *Aucassin et Nicolette* and *Ivain*. These we found delightful as literature. But as literature they did not count, and 'delightful' would have been an unpardonable slip. The only aspect of the course for which something favourable can be said was the obligation, laborious but exacting, to prepare passages to be construed in class. An oral rendering in English or in such French as we could muster was expected of us and our errors were corrected *de vive voix*. I can recall no comments other than detached analytical observations on the vocabulary and its derivation along with some vague references to grammatical forms. From the Introductions we picked up something about the origins of the texts and the scholarship that had produced the editions. My main exertions were absorbed in reading the texts through again and again so as to get my knowledge of them word perfect. This I regard as good. The rest, that is most, of my time was employed in hunting up etymologies for as many words as possible. This I regard as the most laborious and wasteful imposition I have ever endured. It completely destroyed my interest in the course and my respect for those responsible for it. Along with the thousands of other victims of the stupidity of specialists, I had neither the taste nor the gift for such drudgery.

The only serious implication I could perceive in the basic course as presented was what I should now call technical. The technical interest can, it is true, be real for minds of a suitable type. May the devil, the Father of exiles, help the rest! The Middle Ages were conceived as a period when word forms had emerged which might or might not be traceable through intermediary modifications to Classical or Germanic prototypes of a more or less respectable character. The dreary strings of derivatives inscribed on the blackboard represented developments that apparently operated *in vacuo*, isolated from any of the conditions or influences that had given birth, direction or meaning to the modifications exhibited by the formulas in dry white chalk. That the etymologically minded were able to assort these *disjecta membra* into intelligible patterns is little to the point. Even if man were *naturaliter philologus*, he could not live for long on a diet of bits of words. As is only too common, when the specialist insists on teaching the rudiments of his technique in class, the many were sacrificed to the few: the technique, not the text, was being made the object of attention; and for all the bamboozlement about the glory of medieval studies, the scholar was getting out of it by imposing a mere skill.

To complete our bewilderment there were no adequate grammars. Gaston Paris's skilful little résumé was pronounced to be too slight for our purposes. Nyrop's *Grammaire Historique* was advised—a truly magnanimous prescription for beginners! A valiant effort to fill the gap, put together by an English professor of French, raised our hopes only to dash them. The wood, as usual, could not be seen for the trees with all their twigs, tendrils, branches and roots in horrid profusion. We were the babes in that wood.

'So heavy was the emphasis on the linguistic!' as T. G. Glover exclaimed, protesting against similar impositions. 'It was not for the young to criticize, or to ask what Cicero or Homer thought of Grimm's Law. The scholars of those days knew much more grammar than Homer ever knew; and they saw values in grammar and Philology. They were real values, perhaps; but, one dares to say now, they obscured values profounder and more universal.'[1] 'Linguistics stifled literature', says an observer in another field, 'and the Middle Ages eclipsed modern times.'[2] The late Professor Albert Guérard's account of the state of French studies when he went to America in 1906 corroborates what André Chevrillon told me thirty years ago, that when he visited French departments in this country he found most of them in the charge of elderly German philologists whose oral power was negligible.[3] Professor Guérard referred with respect both to philological studies and to his German superiors *d'antan*. I wish to do the same. It was an immense compliment to the leaders of Teutonic scholarship that they should have been invited to dominate with their designs, their methods and their predilections almost the whole range of modern studies in this country and in America. But what this reveals in docility and lack of initiative in our native academic founders I leave to future historians of culture to assess. Anyhow, this vast pedagogical aberration, which queered the pitch for French studies in Anglo-Saxon countries from the start, could drain the subject dry of interest and of value for the

---

[1] T. R. Glover, *The Challenge of the Greek*, p. 16.
[2] Albert Guérard, *Education of a Humanist*, p. 57.
[3] The type is admirably hit off in Dr E. M. W. Tillyard, *The Muse Unchained*, p. 29.

individual student and leave him faced with the quandary of 'Philologie ou rien'. The phrase is Professor Guérard's but I well remember the stalemate it characterizes.

Of the spirit of the Middle Ages—'one of Mankind's rarer achievements' (Toynbee)—not a word was breathed. All that leaked through was childishly disrespectful. It was a period exemplified by a view of the papacy for which Rabelais was our authority. As for its Schoolmen, they could while away their time on those two notorious problems: how many angels could sit on a pin and the dilemma of the donkey faced with equal trusses of hay. I do not mean that our teachers inculcated this sort of thing: they ignored the whole synthesis of medieval thought. Long after my course was over I was brought with a jolt to the discovery that the thirteenth century had been one of the greatest in the history of civilization. But my persistent grievance has been that, after four years' toil on so-called medieval studies, begun on the first day I went to class and ending when I emptied my dust-bin of bits of words into my final scripts and pulled a 'first' out of the litter, no hint was dropped about how a living and present thing like Chartres could have come into existence. Luckily my hard-working father had passed on Hugo's *Notre-Dame de Paris* in translation with the tip to read *that*, ten years before I went to College; so that I had some notion of the romanticized Middle Ages, if not of the real thing. Actually, for the real thing my conviction is that none of my teachers cared a damn; it required something like awe or veneration, which are hardly respectable attitudes in universities bound for the cold sublimities of science. As for the wretched modes of teaching, they are what research will produce if misapplied. Once research gets the bit between its teeth, it lacks horse sense.

Such was the romance of philology as experienced by one of its numerous victims in the first decade of this century.

The last pre-war wave of the high tide of German linguistic science, intrinsically one of the glories of nineteenth-century scholarship, broke in guttural wavelets within our small classroom in the most westerly College in Britain, like the ripples of an ebb-tide in Cardigan Bay. . . .

> But now I only hear
> Its melancholy, long, withdrawing roar,
> Retreating to the breath
> Of the night-wind down the vast edges drear
> And naked shingles of the world.

In telling this story as truthfully as I can recall the few years of miserable grind in my otherwise bountiful education, I must say two things more to prevent misunderstanding and misjudgement. What I was obliged to study was assuredly not the 'Historical Philology: Phonology, Morphology, Syntax, Semantics', proffered by the Prospectus, not one of which ponderous abstractions was ever defined, explained, discussed or illustrated. It was simply and dryly a grubbing for old French words, filched out of Hatzfeld and Darmesteter (if some other hurried seeker had not already bagged the dictionary), and memorized for examination purposes. 'You don't know which they're going to ask,' said a harassed young man to me shortly before my retirement.[1] Fifty years earlier I was obsessed with precisely the same uncertainty. But having accumulated a more than sufficient stock of etymologies, when in my final tests I had finished peppering the old French texts with linguistic observations, I turned on the Renaissance lyrics and gratuitously bespattered them with the rest. This excess of zeal must have helped to secure the class on which hung in dire suspense my subsequent career. It has been a much favoured career. But what

---

[1] Further extravagant examples of the persistence of this abuse have been confided to me since, though not from French studies.

of the foolish virgins who forgot to put enough etymological oil into their untrimmed lamps?

Compulsory philology remained one of the most widely resented components in the modern curriculum until its demands were modified in relation to the rest of the syllabus. I have no wish to prolong the debate here; but I am anxious to acknowledge the difference between studying the history and structure of one's own language and the enforced historical study of early phases of a foreign language which, in its living form, has still largely to be learnt. Great as has been the improvement in the oral use, the reading power of modern language students continues to strike me as inadequate to cope freely with the elaboration and variety of contemporary styles; and I have reason to believe that many good judges outside and within language departments would agree with these reservations. My persistent impression is, I have already said, that only a small proportion of our graduates can be relied on to read modern authors accurately apart, of course, from those whose works they have studied. But my tale is only half told.

Napier's advice on what to do with modern languages was a *non sequitur*. If a proper discipline could not be made out of the study of literature, by what stretch of pedagogical logic was the deficiency to be supplied with the help of the linguistics of that time? If, however, by an unsuspected gift of prescience, Napier foresaw what was going to happen to the teaching of modern literatures, then he was undoubtedly a prophet. Of all aberrations that which derives from the cult and abuse of the history of literature is one I recommend to future historians of undergraduate studies. I have seen much pedagogical mischief in my time. I have endured much and I have indulged in much under compulsion, but with my eyes open. I am seriously relieved to think that better judges than myself among my colleagues affirm that there will be no Dies Irae. That the most infamous of idolatries practised on the young, the substitution of the study of scholars and scholarship for the study of authors and their works, is now rapidly declining in virulence makes much in the recent past appear obtuse, wasteful and unbelievably wrong-headed.

It would be unreasonable to suggest that modern historians have not made indispensable contributions to the study of literature. No self-respecting critic could fail to consult them. But one cannot help feeling in sympathy with those who question or condemn many of the effects their work has produced. The main advantage conceded to the account of interpretative criticism is that the best of it comes infinitely nearer to the spirit of the texts themselves than does the work of the professional historians. Good criticism is rightly claimed as a part of literature, whereas few histories of literature have been produced by men who could even write well. The present danger for the study of literature is that textual and literary critics tend to co-operate with the historians in producing a 'literature' about literature which, under the aegis of teachers themselves interested in the production of scholarship, comes sooner or later to be presented to undergraduates as in itself the principal object of study. What was recently said of the use of works of literary history and criticism in the schools has been true also of the universities at least up to the last ten or twelve years: 'To the inexperienced they contribute the temptation to accept uncritically the ideas of others, to reproduce the judgements of others and to become mentally lazy.'[1]

[1] *Modern Languages* (H.M.S.O., 1956), p. 65. See also p. 43: 'There has comparatively recently been a strong and salutary reaction amongst sixth-form teachers against the survey method of teaching literature in our schools. It is now emphasized that the study of literature should begin with the reading of real literature—the nation's great books—and not criticism or histories of literature.'

Much evidence could be adduced from syllabuses and examination papers—not to call on the resources of memory or on the stock-piles of innumerable theses—of the extent to which in Britain, France, Germany and America the study of the history of literature had from the end of the last century taken precedence over the study of specimens, substituting the problems of literary scholarship for the critical appraisal and even for the careful reading of the texts. Often in my experience as a student (and, I regret to say, during my first twenty years as a lecturer), the piece of literature prescribed played little part in the teaching. I can recall a literature course during the whole year of which no book other than the note-book appeared in the hands either of the professor or of members of his class.[1] It is very probable that hundreds of students in my time and since have answered questions on prescribed books which they had not procured or even set eyes on. It is certain that thousands of answers have been written about texts that were neither prescribed nor read. Many of the answers came straight out of the manuals from which the questions themselves had been taken. Although it was officially *de rigueur* to object to such automatic responses, it has always seemed to me that, logically, the examinees could have claimed they had answered the questions as they were set. How otherwise, for instance, were they to deal with a poser (one out of five!) like: 'Esquisser à larges traits l'histoire de la poésie française au moyen âge'?

In the presentation of French literature the historians have unquestionably played a preponderant and distracting role. Their massive scholarship, their meticulous and exhaustive methods, their external and insensitive approach have exerted

[1] It will be clear from what has been said above that certain texts were studied in class but exclusively for linguistic purposes; and the curiosity is that all the specimens dealt with were chosen to illustrate remote phases of the language. In this limited sense the medievalists set an example which the modernists were slow to apply.

an influence on the study and teaching of the literature of their country which, for all the light it has thrown on circumstance, sequence, derivation and detail, has been on the whole a diversion from, rather than an intensification of, the literary experience itself. It has given us lessons in learned technology, impartial verification and strenuous investigation applied with more conscientiousness than insight or tact. Its main interest has been in the establishment of facts, in documentation, classification and the pursuit and analysis of verbal and ideological influences conceived as data which could be sought out and considered in isolation from the synthesis which is the work itself. A significant feature of the movement and quite a curiosity in the history of French thought about the arts is the fact that taste and its problems were deliberately eschewed, with the result that for fifty years a dominant school of French literary scholars has shown no conspicuous interest in evaluating a masterpiece. Many of its foundations still stand firm and cannot be ignored by the researcher; but the undergraduate should be warned not to stray too far along its precise and divagating labyrinths. From the first the work of the school was much nearer to science than to aesthetics, nearer, that is, to the preatomic science of measurement without mystery.[1] And it has come as a relief to the intelligent reader and still more to the *fin bec* to find that the domination of this phase of powerful extraversion and superannuated rationalism is now being seriously challenged even in its stronghold.

The most influential leader of the historical movement, Gustave Lanson, had foreseen some of the dangers with which the teaching of literature was threatened by the

[1] 'En attendant (the reference is to the early decades of this century) l'enseignement supérieur s'efforçait d'aligner toutes les disciplines, histoire, études littéraires, psychologie, sociologie, sur les méthodes de la science.' P.-H. Simon, *Histoire de la littérature française au XXe siècle*, Alcan, 1955.

advancement of the type of scholarship he so vigorously proposed and practised. To direct effectively the attention of the young and to protect their interests, he recommended a method of commentary which has since become famous as *l'explication française*. But for fifty years the *lecture expliquée* (as it was popularly called) has played an inferior role—in my own experience an infinitesimal role—compared with the assimilation and regurgitation by pupils and students of the content of the manuals, for the outstanding example of which Lanson himself was responsible.

It is of doubtful benefit to a nation's literature to produce a text-book so competent as Lanson's *Histoire de la littérature française*. The first edition dates from 1894. A betting man would run no risk in wagering that for the last half century not a single work out of the whole sequence of French literature, not even *Le Bourgeois Gentilhomme*, has been so widely read, so frequently consulted and so carefully memorized as that stout, closely printed, roughly bound, unalluring, but oh! how convenient tome. How could it be otherwise when, to confirm the mischief, Lanson and his contemporaries, Faguet and Brunetière, figured so repeatedly in the question-papers that even in the examination room, they were infinitely nearer the toiling candidates—bowing over them in sympathy, whispering in their memories, prompting their phrases—than were the invigilators, who could do nothing to prevent the collusion? Though distant or dead in the flesh, Lanson, Faguet and Brunetière were there in spirit and in truth. But as modern universities have no interest in spirits and no eyes for truth except when it is scientific, the subtle intruders could not possibly have been detected even by members of the most subtle of the faculties. It was difficult when I was an undergraduate to resist the thought that the originals had been written to provide occasions for the late nineteenth-century linguists and historians to exhibit their *maîtrise* and to impose their methods. The scholars loomed much too large in the schemes of study and in the way the schemes were presented. They dominated the stage and the authors were their understudies. As for the figures in the texts, Charlemagne, Roland, Oliver, Turpin were always in danger of disappearing behind the importunate erudites, some of them men of irascible self-importance who have by now faded off the records. For thousands of undergraduates Roland is irrevocably dead—and so by poetic justice and the march of scholarship are his undertakers. As for Rabelais, Ronsard, Du Bellay and Montaigne, who could resist dear old Faguet's portraits of them and his version of their works? Lanson was found everywhere, his familiar form standing in front of the poets, prose-writers and playwrights, ordering the long tradition like a non-commissioned officer drilling an awkward squad of Artists' Rifles. What a relief it was a few years ago to watch Dr Geoffrey Brereton, like a gentle avenging angel, redeeming the 'attardés et égarés' whom Lanson's interdiction had suppressed for sixty years.[1]

Dr Brereton's action reminds us that after all there are 'good interpreters' (in Tristan Bernard's sense), and that critics and scholars can help to introduce and recommend the good things of literature. They may even correct and refurbish our judgements so long as they don't thrust themselves to the front of the boards, talk long and learnedly *à la cantonade* and, in the opinion of thousands of young men and women waiting to be interested, earn the reputation of being *raseurs*.

A last word. I have admitted that the syllabus I studied contained some good texts. Among them were the Essays of Montaigne, or rather a selection as tame as could be contrived out of the first brief 'chapters', but for the inclusion of

[1] Geoffrey Brereton, *An Introduction to the French Poets*, Methuen, 1956.

that pedagogical time-bomb, the essay on Education with its insistence on the training of the judgement. The paper-back edition we used contained a rough woodcut of the Essayist, his head round and bald, a little like the face of the full moon with faintly ironical eyes and an indulgent expression. Often I used to think that moonlike visage was poised behind the chair of our teacher, smiling down indulgently, ironically on his efforts and on ours. And in the fifty years that have elapsed I have sometimes turned my head to see if the same luminous phiz was not casting a silver ray of warning and of sympathy over my shoulder at some bewildered young Jones or other in the class I was trying to teach.

III

THE ASSAULT ON FRENCH LITERATURE

'Ce qu'il demande, c'est *la réduction de la littérature à l'histoire.*' La phrase, qui est de M. Lanson, mérite qu'on s'y arrête, car elle donne la clef de presque toute son évolution'.

—P. Leguay, *Universitaires d'Aujourd'hui*, 1912

Not many years ago a distinguished alumnus of an Irish university left on a senior common-room table a collection of examination papers which offered a moment's distraction. Suddenly a question seemed to flatter yet mystify one's memory. To a paragraph of translator's English extolling the virtues of a French poet was appended the injunction: 'Give Lanson's words for this.' The candidates had evidently been expected to memorize a paragraph from the famous History of French Literature and to reproduce it verbatim. Lanson had superseded Vigny as the object of literary study; his manual had become a sacred text, a breviary to be mumbled over before matins.

For more than half a century—though with diminishing pressure of late—the presentation of the national literature to young learners in France and to thousands of pupils and students abroad has been dominated by the directives, methods and examples of a powerful school of historians whose founder, Gustave Lanson, died in 1934, to be succeeded in the esteem of serious readers and researchers by Daniel Mornet.

In the allied field of comparative studies, widely exploited during the Lanson régime, the senior name was that of Fernand Baldensperger; though, to express a partiality, the *comparatiste* whose thought and writing has given most pleasurable reward was Paul Hazard, who died during the Occupation.

Beyond these almost contemporary masters rise in grateful retrospect the contrasted figures of a couple of academic critics, nearly exact coevals until 1906—one surviving the other by a decade, to be himself outlived by the vivacity of some of his works, which still attract the beginner and stimulate the connoisseur. Few students of the French Renaissance for the last fifty years can have been able to resist Faguet's chapters on *le bon* Rabelais, *le gentil* Clément, the poets of the Pléiade or the Essays of Montaigne. If in my student days the familiar charm of Faguet's manner tended to distract us from the originals, the genial commentator certainly contrived to give us the literary personalities he chatted about in far more palpable outlines than our laborious fumblings could evoke from their records. (How well I remember preparing to translate Rabelais' storm extravaganza into nautical English and fretting over etymological fluctuations in that period of slippery linguistics!)

At the antipodes from the impressionism of Faguet, Ferdinand Brunetière had striven to systematize his notions of literary evolution. Echoes of his oratory rang in our ears as we read his studies of the Classical literature, strewn with *qui*'s and *que*'s, such as might have punctuated the rhetoric of the great preachers whom he admired. Impressionism or systematization, which were we to choose?

There in our wallets lay the touchstone and talisman, the true foundation for the study of French literature, the twelve hundred sere and yellow leaves of Lanson's *Histoire*, a book which inspired antipathy in my youth because of the importance officially attached to it, reinforced by what I took to be its abstract stodginess and lack of line and colour. Philosophic age has corrected that notion and brought respect for the most remarkable history of a nation's literature ever to be crushed into one uncomely but ineluctable tome. Yet nothing would seem to have been further from Lanson's expressed purpose than to attempt to supplant the study of literature by that of literary history. His case is curious and more ambiguous than his pronouncements appear to make it; while his situation during and after the turn of the century had so marked an incidence on the development of literary studies—not only in France—that it repays attention, all the more because of the care with which the scrupulous scholar analysed his reactions at critical moments of his subsequent career.

His book is formally offered in an old-fashioned phrase to whoever reads French writers. To pupils in the *lycées* and to students in the faculties it is recommended as being all the more useful because it has not been written exclusively to serve their purposes; it has not been 'measured to fit an examination', but is addressed to all cultivated minds who wish to broaden their study of literature in a disinterested way. The point is driven home: students will be the better prepared for their examinations if they can forget that they are candidates, and study literature for its own sake. The teaching and study of literature, Lanson complains, has been jeopardized by turning it into a pabulum for syllabuses, to be assimilated as quickly as possible so as to prevent the candidate from being 'ploughed', and then to be discarded for ever. The habit of teaching and learning *everything* has led to a literal knowledge devoid of literary virtue. Literature is reduced to a dry collection of facts and formulas such as fill young minds with disgust for the works themselves. This pedagogic error depends on another, deeper and more general. Through a fatal superstition, for which neither science itself nor its representatives are responsible, the attempt has been made to impose a scientific form on literature and to esteem literature only for what elements of positive knowledge it contains. For this mistake Lanson blames a phrase dashed off by Renan in his early enthusiasm for science: 'L'étude de l'Histoire littéraire est destinée à remplacer en grande partie la lecture directe des œuvres de l'esprit humain.' What could be more forceful than Lanson's rejoinder? In literature as in art, he says, you cannot eliminate the work itself which is the repository and revelation of the individual. If the reading of original texts is not the perpetual illustration and the final end of literary history, the latter can but provide the kind of knowledge which is sterile and valueless. Such progress leads us back to the worst defects of the Middle Ages, when only summa and manuals were known. It was the virtue of the Renaissance to reject the gloss in favour of the text.

How regrettable that Lanson could not have controlled pedagogical practice and the vices of examiners in accordance with such wise distinctions! Some of the dangers of the scientific attitude he sees plainly, but not others; and despite the decision of his words, his mind wavers, as we shall see, between the claims of erudition and those of 'impressionism'. The study of literature, he continues, cannot today progress without erudition: a certain amount of exact, positive knowledge is necessary to serve as basis and guide to our judgement. Nor is anything more legitimate than the attempt made, through the application of scientific methods, to link up our ideas and our particular impressions in an effort to represent synthetically [sic] the march, the expansions and the transformations of literature. But two things must be kept in sight: the object of literary history is the description of individualities; it is based on individual intuitions. The true aim is not a species but Corneille or Hugo. Neither the object nor the means of literary knowledge is, in the strict sense, scientific. That is to say, literature is not an object of knowledge: it is experience, taste, enjoyment. It is not something to be *known*; something to be *learnt*; it is to be cultivated and loved. Those mathematicians who amuse themselves with literature and who go to the theatre or pick up a book for recreation are nearer the truth than the *littérateurs* who don't *read* but *plunder* and who think their job is done when they have converted into *fiches* all the print they can lay their hands on. The italics are Lanson's. The passage should have been printed in red letters as a warning to his disciples.

At this point the argument takes a turn which is particularly worth notice: a kind of ideologue speaks. Literature, he continues, is designed to give us intellectual pleasure; its supreme excellence is that it habituates us to take pleasure in ideas. It provides relaxation after professional tasks; it lifts the mind above professional prejudices; it 'humanizes' the specialists. More than ever before people need to be touched by philosophy. But the technical study of philosophy is not accessible to all. Literature is in the noblest sense a vulgarization of philosophy, the medium through which pass into society all the great philosophical currents which determine the progress or at least the changes of society. Literature keeps alive in souls otherwise oppressed by the exigencies of life and submerged under material preoccupations that disturbing interest in important questions which directs life and gives it a meaning and an end. For many of our colleagues, religion has vanished; science is remote. Through literature alone can come those solicitations which lift them above narrow egoism and brutalizing toil.

The History, far from showing any rigour or excess of method, is often personal and impressionistic in tone, as, for example, in the pages on Renan; its writing was largely inspired, if the term may be used, by antipathy to the systematic approach of Taine. The only 'method' perceptible is an emphasis on the extraction of ideas; Lanson is most at ease with texts that are rich in ideas of a rational cast. As a thinker he appears to belong to that line of modern *têtes fortes* who proceed from the Enlightenment and who prefer minds of their own type—clear-headed intellectuals, critical, logical, humane, agnostic. Not intuitive, but respectful of traditional standards of taste.

Lanson's impartiality makes him a kind of *philosophe* without a philosophy, a typical modern academic in his avoidance of convictions except for the belief in method. Intelligence is his conspicuous talent; he is safe but limited in feeling. What intuitions he possessed never reached beyond the scope of his reason. But his intelligence is aware of its limits and his work is incompatible with pretensions. The misfortune for the millions of his readers has been his lack of sensibility—conspicuously his lack of the type of sensibility characteristic of his period. He rarely succeeds with what since the Romantics is meant by a 'poet'. Ignoring Mallarmé's advice to Degas, he looks for ideas in every piece of verse he picks up. Not that he often considers anything so insignificant as a verse: the solid wall of his prose rarely sports a petal. Yet if a feeling can be transmuted into an idea, if an *idée émotive* can be reduced to an *idée tout court*, his intelligence and his impartiality enable him to say things that are admirably sound. Ill at ease with Hugo, he is yet not shy of him. He begins by being as obtuse as Faguet about Hugo's lack of ideas. But if the reader persists, intimations of the perplexing qualities of that great myth-maker-turned-mystery-monger's imagination seep through the balanced account he offers of Hugo's unbalanced gifts. Read his Hugo by all means, but pass quickly over his Baudelaire to whose sensibility Lanson gives a school-master's nought. Don't miss his portrait of Remy de Gourmont. Gourmont, a *libertin* astray in the hot-house of Symbolist *mysticité*, meets a critic who appreciates his alert but superficial mind, and Lanson finds his level as a writer.

The style, terse, *terne*, incisive, with which he marks the principal *étapes* in the vast movement of French literature is that of a superior accountant, the vigilant keeper of the literary records of a nation. He sits like Madame at the desk of Lapérouse: all the sharp competence of the masterful *caissière* is his. The *maître-chef* of course is out of sight. He too is French, but of another order of greatness, the humblest of the masters of taste. Like the correct lady at the desk, the historian of French literature shows no interest in taste; his concern is with facts. The variegated cornucopia of French styles flourishes on a consol beyond: you must risk a *gaminerie* to capture a plum.

Beside the foreword to the first edition, Lanson left some notable pronouncements on questions of method. A glance at one or two of them will assure us that his mind was far from rigid and his thought on method anything but negligible, although it continues to fluctuate, as did the criticism of his time, between the demands of 'science', to which he is empirically addicted, and those of 'impressionism', which experience tells him cannot be ignored. Delivered in 1904 when he succeeded the unillustrious Larroumet in the Chair of French Eloquence at Paris, his inaugural lecture reveals that he had found the first signs of good method in his predecessor's thesis on Marivaux. The discriminations he makes are worth noticing. In reaction from the systematizing tendencies of Taine and Brunetière, Larroumet is depicted as having concentrated on the object of his study, the text, without passing beyond it. In equally strong reaction from impressionism, he was not content to read a book, close it and give his impression of it and its author. He chose the slow but sure way of collecting all the documents useful to throw light on the work and to determine its character; and he limited and submitted the subjective reactions of taste strictly to the contents of the work studied. Preferring to make deductions slowly from a multiplicity of facts, Larroumet was satisfied if his personal feelings conformed to collective tradition or to the feelings of another individual. His habit of citing secondary works by unknown authors or young people, 'without interest assuredly', is commended as an example of his concern for exact and minute information. Against the 'enormity' of his thesis the Faculty protested, complaining that its size was 'a little out of proportion to the importance and nature of the subject'. It was, said one malicious person, like placing 'an elephant on a butterfly'.

Lanson scoffs at the notion that the format of a study should be made to match the 'aesthetic colour' of the author who is its subject, and claims that his predecessor had, like himself, acquired the better method from his training at the École Normale. 'It is simply', he says, 'the historical method. The minuteness of the study, the weight of the book are not faults in a doctor's thesis, which is not written for people of society'. . . The distinction he makes is logical; but the preference it emphasizes, while it has promoted much scholarly activity, has been unfortunate and sometimes even disastrous in ways for which Lanson could not be held directly responsible. The bias in favour of an erudition which has become competitive and remunerative has widened into a serious diversion of interest from literature itself.

Having denounced impressionistic criticism, the historian finds himself obliged to admit that 'impressionism is the only method which gives us contact with beauty'; and he continues with less enthusiasm than caution: 'Employ it then for this purpose frankly, but limit it to this purpose forcibly. ... Let us distinguish *savoir* from *sentir*, and what we can know from what we must feel; let us refuse to feel when we can know; let us not think we know when we feel. I really believe that this sums up the scientific method in the history of literature.' Then comes a curious remark: 'The history of literature benefits from the slightly disdainful opinion which men who could do it harm have of it. (Men of church and state are implied.) Their indifference to our innocent games assures our liberty.' The 'scientific' attitude is non-committal; the historian of literature is not *engagé*, and the young are left without directives.

Having thus made obeisance to impressionism which he seems to regard as a foible, if not as a flaw, in human nature, the lecturer concludes with a confession (by proxy) of the excesses of the impressionistic type: '*Nous avons été trop artistes, trop acrobates*, persuaded in our vanity that readers do not come to us to learn about Montaigne or romanticism but to see us perform . . .'

Lanson was no doubt right to prefer his ideal of the historical scholar to the type of impressionistic 'critic' that pullulated around him. In practice, however, the values attaching to his ideal have been cultivated only too exclusively and have ended in a veritable cult of exhaustive erudition, as if the accumulation and regimentation of facts have of themselves a power of arbitration in literary studies such as would not be claimed for statistics even by the most rigorous social scientist. 'The researcher's task', Lanson declares, 'is to furnish all the facts, all the materials for the discussion, all the solutions to the complete and precise knowledge of the subject.' The vapidity of impressionism, we see, is being displaced by the *mystique* of omniscient research.

That such a conception has led to vast increases in circumstantial knowledge about literature is undeniable.[1] But the spirit of literature has retreated before the drive of a process which is not content to collect but must *display* all the facts of the case. In France more even than in Britain the gap between scholarship and criticism has become dangerously wide.[2]

Lanson praises his predecessor for having drawn all his ideas from texts and documents in complete freedom from doctrinal issues: 'he brought only his method and his judgement'. Judgement, we should note, of one kind only, that which is applicable to the method extolled. Judgements of value are never mentioned: they would doubtless be 'doctrinal'. As for imagination, 'Larroumet imagines only as he judges: the document may require "vision" to interpret it, but where the document ceases, the vision must stop.' After commenting as if apologetically on the lighter side of his predecessor's review articles and conversation, Lanson says with evident approval that from the moment Larroumet functioned as a teacher he was not the same man: *il ne jouait plus*. 'One might say', he adds, 'that Larroumet felt his own teachers looking over his shoulder and repressing all literary velleities' . . .

The words evoke a sombre amphitheatre crowded with students listening to one of a series of lectures packed with minute references masterfully arranged but treated mechanic-

[1] Circumstantial but by no means useless. I do not wish to make reservations about scholarship as such but to insist on the misplaced emphasis on erudite, at the expense of literary, interests.

[2] No one appeared to regret this more than Daniel Mornet who claimed to remember a time when there was no opposition between history and criticism, and who maintained that they are not contradictory activities. See his note on the sixtieth anniversary of the Société de l'Histoire littéraire de la France, *Revue de l'Histoire*, January–March, 1953. But Mornet's work offers no bridge. Look at his treatment of poetry!

ally without a touch of intensity or feeling. The complete absence of humour was for one member of the audience who was Welsh, somehow impressive. But where was that *éclat*, that flash of wit in touch with lively or lovely things, where was the *esprit de finesse* to balance the *esprit de géomètre*, the pinch of gallic salt or Rabelaisian verve which had turned Renaissance learning into a gay science? The hard voice of the literary historian ground on, making a mortar of facts.

My recollection is not of Larroumet or of Lanson; but here is a passage from Péguy's *Cahiers* which supports my impression.[1] It hits off the characteristic *mélange* of competence, precision and irrelevance in the master's manner:

I was at the École Normale just when M. Lanson came to teach there. I can recall as if I were there now the long, punctilious, serious lessons on the history of the French theatre which plunged us into a stupor of admiration. I speak without the least irony. I have no desire to laugh, believe me. That was work! He had read and he knew all that had been published or played, or both, in connection with the theatre in France up to Corneille. And as lessons they were admirable in composition and in sequence. A close-knit fabric. Everything held together. He knew all about it. And everything was known. If this man had written an *Iphigénie* it was because he was the great-nephew of the uncle of the man who had sketched a play of that name, and he had found that very sketch in the papers of his son-in-law. In one case things were explained by the playwrights, in another by the players or by the gazette or by the trestles. Now it was the fault of the court, now of the town; now the king's attendants were to blame (and perhaps the king himself); at another time the fault lay with the bourgeois of the Marais. Besides, the Church or the bishop might pick a quarrel with the players. Anyhow, all

[1] I am indebted to Dr W. G. Moore of St John's College, Oxford, for this passage from Péguy's *Cahiers de la quinzaine* (9e cahier, XIVe série, 27 avril 1913). The translation is mine.

was 'taped'. The history of the French theatre was known. It was a history that unwound like a ball of thread. The great achievement was laid out before us, bound hand and foot.

To return to Lanson's words. Here is the 'method' tabulated (I translate literally):

What is this writer?—biography, psychology, aesthetic or social tendency. What is this work?—its place in a genre, a group, a movement; then, in this group, genre, movement, its nuance or special quality? . . . Larroumet will have his place at the foot of a page or in the bibliographical notices, not as a writer to be studied, but as a guide, instrument and help for students. He has left some superior examples of inductive criticism, purged of apriorism and of fantasy, in which intelligence, taste, wit and talent are all subordinated to the facts and are applied strictly to bringing out the value of the contents of the documents. He has shown us the way. . . .

The strait and narrow way to the reference library or the 'stack room', but it has not led the student to Paradise or to literature.

Let us take a deep breath and rise, if we can, to the level of that remark of Coleridge's quoted by Sir Herbert Read: 'The terms system, method, science, are mere improprieties of courtesy, when applied to a mass enlarging by endless appositions, but without a nerve that oscillates, or a pulse that throbs, in sign of growth or inward sympathy.'[1]

The efforts made in France during the latter half of the nineteenth century to apply scientific methods to the criticism of literature attracted wide attention. But their success was persistently jeopardized by the crudity of the conceptions behind them, drawn for the most part from the physical sciences as understood by literary or semi-literary

[1] *The True Voice of Feeling*, p. 170.

minds. Lanson was right to point out in a speech at the University of Brussels that no branch of science 'condemned itself' to reproducing the external plan, or to using the formulas, of another science. Nor should the literary scholar attempt to copy the modes of study or to appropriate the language of chemistry and natural history. These remarks were aimed at Taine.

A brilliant, energetic mind, diverted from philosophy when his thesis for the Doctorate was rejected by examiners whom he subsequently flayed, Hippolyte Taine had in 1864 published a notable *History of English Literature*. The Introduction to this work was devoted to the dogmatic exposition of a form of criticism modelled on scientific notions, hastily taken over from contemporary naturalistic theories and fitted into a schema of the critic's fabrication.

What mischief has not been done to generations of students approaching French literature (and to many of their teachers examining them on it) by the set of deterministic formulas which Taine's 'system' stamped on their retentive memories! Taine himself frequently forgot his theories. His mind leapt from the abstract to the concrete and back again with mercurial velocity. Before a concrete case—a man, a book, a scene in nature or in a salon, a painted canvas or a violent deed—he could apply to each an incisive, logical but colourful style, and to such effect that many of his essays still offer brisk and stimulating reading compared with which Lanson's solid prose looks dull. In striking contrast to the deterministic clauses of the Introduction, Taine's *History of English Literature* concludes with an emphatic assertion of personal taste. An incredibly melodramatic outburst in praise of his favourite poet ends with the words: 'I prefer Alfred de Musset to Tennyson.'

Objections were raised at once to Taine's scientific theorizings. Sainte-Beuve made judicious reservations. But

Taine was irrepressible; his contemporaries found it hard to resist his confident versatility, his undeniable seriousness, the glint and force of his style. Even if he had too rapidly synthesized a few bold notions derived from the study of zoological specimens, among which man was classified as a 'gorille féroce et lubrique', it could not be denied that his inoculation of criticism with scientific theory had 'caught on'. Sainte-Beuve himself, while condemning Taine's excesses took care to point out that he too had attempted to be scientific in a manner befitting a critic who had begun as a student of medicine.

For Lanson at the beginning of this century, Taine, though dead for over a decade, was still an embarrassment, an active thorn in the flesh. In trying to infuse criticism with science, he had brilliantly bungled the job. Those scientific fictions of his had to be disqualified, liquidated, quashed, and their débris removed from the sight of the young, before the true theory of scientific history, as applied to literature, could be proclaimed with expectations of acceptance and applause. This Lanson set out to do in a lecture delivered at the University of Brussels in 1909 on the subject of *L'Esprit scientifique et la méthode de l'histoire littéraire*.[1] The idea of a 'scientific' method of literary history had hardened in his mind and his differentiation of it from Taine's system of false analogies is presented in clear and simple terms. He rejects all efforts to model a technique on scientific theories or laboratory practices and adopts and recommends the attitude of the scientist and the guidance of the scientific spirit. When he comes to define his own method, it is found to be indistinguishable from the moral attitude and logical

[1] This lecture appeared in the *Revue de l'Université de Bruxelles*, December–January 1910. It is collected in G. Lanson: *Méthodes de l'histoire littéraire*, Éditions Les Belles Lettres, 1 January 1925. I shall refer to it subsequently as 'Brussels'.

practice of the rational scholar. His conception of literature, however, is another matter and lacks differentiation. He seems content to revert to the stock formula of Renaissance poetics. Having Taine's analogies still on his mind, he deplores 'the identification of the literary genre, *which is sustained by imitation*, with the living species which is perpetuated by generation'.[1] We see what a devitalized conception underlies his protest. Whether poets are born or made, literature, in contradistinction to living things, is sustained by imitation. Then, having settled the fallacies of Taine with this fustian tenet, Lanson turns in the right direction and points to the superior model: 'We should admire (*aimer*) and imitate the discretion of Sainte-Beuve. He could appreciate what science is; he knew what a fact is.' But he didn't compare his work to that of Lamarck: 'Voilà notre maître, Messieurs.'[2] And Lanson urges his audience to follow the road Sainte-Beuve pointed out. 'Our way of participating in the scientific life,' he continues, 'the only mode of life that doesn't deceive, is to develop in ourselves the scientific spirit.'

It would be useful if, at this point, the reader could turn to a curious little collection of critical tit-bits put together by Fernand Baldensperger and an American colleague under the pretentious title of *La Critique et l'Histoire littéraire en France*.[3] There he would find a few paragraphs in which Lanson criticizes Sainte-Beuve for his biographical leanings:

He has not treated the masterpieces of literary art any differently than he treated the hastily composed memoirs of a general or a woman's epistolary effusions; all this type of writing he puts to the same use; he uses it as leverage to get at the soul or the mind: *c'est précisément éliminer la qualité littéraire*.[4]

[1] Brussels, p. 23. My italics.
[2] Loc. cit. Cf. 'Nous n'étions pas embarrassés pour nous choisir un saint'. From a lecture on Sainte-Beuve (*Revue de Belgique*, 2ᵉ série, 1905).
[3] Brentano's, 1945.   [4] My italics.

This was written in 1895, and comes from the avant-propos to a collection of studies which Lanson published in that year. It reveals an entirely different attitude to Sainte-Beuve from that arrived at in 1909, and the difference reflects a profound change in Lanson's mind. He was on the way to becoming very much the kind of 'critic' he had disapproved of in Sainte-Beuve. He will, to a greater extent than Sainte-Beuve, eliminate literary quality from his main interests and objectives.

Baldensperger admits that the word 'probity' applies to Lanson 'in all the force of the term and in all senses of the word'. The honesty of his intentions is not in question here, and nothing invidious is implied when we say he changed his mind. But in reacting against his predecessors Lanson had become obsessed with what Baldensperger calls 'a rigorous accentuation of "method"', which the least literary-minded of his disciples took over and armed themselves with'. Baldensperger ends his brief note by remarking that, under the influence of the Dreyfus Affair, Lanson became 'rationalist' and 'voltairian'; and he points to some of the defects of judgement which he thinks this development produced in the famous History of French Literature.

It seems clear that in the first decade of this century Lanson's preoccupations underwent an important change. His primary interest in literature—genuine so far as it could be in a man whose reason was keener than his sensibility—yielded in large measure to a type of literary history which he confessed to be motivated by the spirit of science. But the irreducible impressionism that had characterized his earlier work[1] persists as a kind of afterthought and comes recur-

[1] His chief literary monographs were published in a little over half a decade: *Bossuet* (1891), *Boileau* (1892), *Corneille* (1898). The first edition of the *Histoire de la Littérature française* appeared in 1894; it contains many impressionistic judgements. The study of Nivelle de la Chaussée had appeared in 1887. But the *Voltaire* of 1906 shows a very different spirit from that of any of its predecessors.

THE ASSAULT ON FRENCH LITERATURE 43

rently into conflict with his growing obsession with the science of history. These dual allegiances we shall watch struggling in his thought during and after the critical year 1909. They find expression in his discourses and articles on method as well as in the solid works of bibliography that occupied his later years.

I have called 1909 the critical year because it was then that issues were joined in public. Lanson delivered his address at the University of Brussels on *L'Esprit scientifique et la méthode de l'histoire littéraire*, and he and Gustave Rudler opened a conference of secondary language teachers at the Musée Pédagogique in Paris on the subject of *L'Enseignement du français*.[1] At this meeting specific charges were made against the modes of teaching French in the *lycées*. From the vehemence of the attacks and the acerbity of some of the asides and innuendoes, which spared neither the *professeurs de lycée* nor, by implication, certain university professors *en vue*, we must conclude that the teaching of the native language and the study of the national literature were, at the beginning of this century, in a serious state of depression. A violent revulsion is evinced by the speakers from what, with monotonous frequency, they call 'impressionism'. The term is rarely defined; but what they usually imply by it is the contemporary state of the use of literature in the training of taste. This they accuse of having degenerated into a kind of pedantic dilettantism. Elsewhere at this time Lanson characterizes the subject of modern French literature as 'the theatre of all the fantasies, the battlefield of all the passions and, let it be said in a whisper, the refuge of all kinds of laziness. Everyone feels himself competent to speak of it the

---

[1] *Conférence du Musée Pédagogique*, 1909: *L'Enseignement du français*. Par MM. G. Lanson, G. Rudler, A. Cahen, J. Bézard. Paris: Imprimerie Nationale. Lanson led off with some characteristic remarks on 'La Crise de Méthodes'.

moment he finds he has sufficient wit or is conscious of enthusiasm or hatred; and many of those who like literature think of "method" as a scarecrow. They believe they have to defend their pleasures and their turn of mind from its mortifying tyranny.'[1] Such anxieties, he assures his readers, are chimerical.

Against the presumed egoism of the professor of taste Lanson reacts frequently and sharply: 'We want him to devote himself wholly to making his subject known', he says in a footnote to the same article, 'and not to use it for the purpose of showing himself off to advantage. *Inde ira*.'[2] The implication of these protests is that only too often the personality of the teacher is flaunted before his youthful audience to their amusement or boredom. They learn nothing of value and leave with no extension of positive knowledge. Worst of all they have never heard of 'method'. But to point this out is to infuriate the 'spécialistes de la légèreté',[3] by which is meant the teachers: *Inde ira*.

The logical force of delivery, the outspoken challenge, the verbal flaying right and left, high and low, the strength of conviction are unusual for an academic in office to display. Just as the vigilance with which Lanson pursues every aspect of the problem that strikes him as in need of support or of specific illustration—or even of downright condemnation—is in its way admirable. It reveals a commendable anxiety for the efficiency of higher education, a concern on the level of authority of a kind we could do with today. Except that

---

[1] This quotation comes from an article called 'Histoire littéraire', which was brought to my notice by Dr. W. G. Moore. A note by the author informs us that it was composed in 1909 and revised in 1910, when it appeared in the *Revue du Mois* (10 October). The article was reprinted as Lanson's contribution to a collection called *La Méthode dans les Sciences*, II, edited by E. Borel and published by Alcan in 1911. There is some overlapping between this article and the Brussels speech.

[2] *Histoire littéraire*, p. 262, note.   [3] Ibid., p. 258.

today the direction of the argument might have to be reversed: only too much scientific method has been applied to the presentation of humane subjects, and far too much literary history has been substituted for the direct approach to texts. If what Baldensperger called 'l'histoire littéraire méthodique *à la Lanson*' has proved a rigorous and useful model of investigation, its influence on teaching is far from having been beneficial to those who have wished to *read* French literature with appreciation and enjoyment, whether at home or abroad. A fatal distinction has arisen between intelligent reading, which should give pleasure in the texts themselves, and *studying*, which has often meant the enforced application of the methods and instruments of scholarship to texts whose values the reader has not had time to appraise.

Lanson's methodological pronouncement seems to me one of the most erroneous programmes for the study and teaching of literature that has ever been propounded. Showing an almost complete *volte-face* in its author's attitude, it reveals certain fallacies especially inimical to the presentation of French literature which, in one form or another and in varying, if diminishing, degrees, have remained virulent or endemic up to the present. Lanson's propaganda for literary history as a scientific discipline and the energy and precision of his injunctions and protests enable us to trace these aberrations back to their source in the thought and example of a most active scholar and teacher, whose influence on the conception and modes of French literary studies was for the first third of this century almost universal in authority.

'Notre méthode est donc essentiellement la méthode historique,'[1] he affirms, making no claim to the invention, but citing the names of eminent historians, Langlois, Seignobos and Monod, who had produced methodological theories which he regarded as models. But what is the object

[1] *Histoire littéraire*, p. 224.

of the new method when applied to the study of literature? The answer is typical: 'Like all kinds of history, literary history strives to attain general facts, to dissociate representative facts, and to mark the connection (*l'enchaînement*) between general and representative facts.'[1]

Is it possible to think of a more abstract approach to literature or to conceive of a more impersonal or more generalized objective to its study? It seems clear that the man who could use these words with deliberate intent was no longer concerned with literature as a living mode of intrinsic experience and value. Lanson had become absorbed in his own conception of literary history and was henceforth to be mainly interested in promoting a kind of historiography founded on the application of a rational, scientific method to literary material. That this has produced useful results in basic factual scholarship is not being questioned here. Lanson was justified in the claim he made at Brussels that during the past twenty years 'la masse de la connaissance solide s'est considérablement accrue'.[2] What I consider regrettable is that he should have tried to impose on the student of literature, not only the method but the attitude of mind characteristic of the scientific historian, having apparently assumed that this method and attitude constituted a superior mode of training even for the undergraduate.

This aberration has led to abuse and aridity rather than to illumination. It has produced, in many cases, a divorce of genuine interest from the values that are found in literature and has often ended in disruption of contact with the life of great texts. However justifiable his attack on the decadent régime of academic taste, Lanson seems not to have perceived —not at least in his moments of scientific fervour—that he was raising up a barrier of rational hurdles and exercises between the student and the object of any attraction he might

[1] *Histoire littéraire*, p. 224.   [2] Brussels, p. 35.

feel for the content or spirit of good books. In short, Lanson and his disciples seem at this time united in the negative belief that in the *lycées* as well as in the universities, literary texts should be studied for any but literary purposes.

Method then is for Lanson the first essential, and we have heard him admit that for many teachers his insistence threatened to turn method into a scarecrow. There is abundant evidence to show that, at this time, both Lanson and Rudler were fanatical methodologists. Rudler in his speech at the Musée Pédagogique went so far as to identify the whole of education with method.[1] And there can be little doubt that much language-literature work since their time has been impaired by the pedagogical excess for which the French themselves have a useful formula: the cult of *la méthode méthodisante*. The phrase has its counterpart in that proverbial misnomer beloved of British academics: 'training the mind'.

The new critical spirit treats all literature, including dogmatic criticism *à la* Brunetière, as material for scientific investigation, prompted by the negative ideal of eliminating every possibility of personal error: 'L'esprit critique est un esprit scientifique averti, qui ne se fie pas à la rectitude naturelle de nos facultés pour trouver la vérité, et qui règle ses démarches sur l'idée des erreurs à éviter.'[2] That sounds final. But at other times a timorous secondary motif will appear, intimating acceptance of the inevitable 'reactions of aesthetic sentiment' as appertaining to the nature of the literary experience itself: '... il y aura toujours dans nos études une part fatale et légitime d'impressionnisme'.[3] The reservation sounds like a recantation, but it is really a sign of vacillation on the part of an honest mind, still sensitive to

[1] 'Il n'y a d'éducatif que la méthode à condition, bien entendu, de la pratiquer soi-même.'
[2] *Histoire littéraire*, p. 229.   [3] Brussels, p. 29.

irruptions from a split allegiance. Yet there was no withdrawal from a fixed attitude. Either the power of 'individual modification', which Lanson still recognized as part of the reaction of the historian of literature, was not a strong enough element in his own make-up, or—and this is more likely—having become absorbed in purely 'scientific' occupations, he was content to rely on secondhand verdicts, as this aside suggests: 'We will renounce the use of our own impression only on condition that we adopt that of a forerunner or of a colleague . . .'[1] What is remarkable here is the explicit indifference on the part of a professor of literature to expressing and defending his own taste. Lanson, I am afraid, has been the patron of a long line of literary eunuchs.

To support his argument he finds it necessary to distinguish between knowing and feeling. He expends much energy on trying to draw the line without, apparently, being able to convince himself that the distinction can be justified. A complete separation of knowing from feeling would of course be fatal to the study of literature, and this Lanson has grudgingly to admit. 'Does not literature, by its definition, enclose us in impressionism?'[2] he asks. The development he gives to this point is both cautious and depressing. 'In any case,' he continues, 'the danger for us is that we should use our imagination instead of our observation and think we know when we are only feeling. Historians are not safe from this danger, but the documents they work on don't expose them to it in the same degree: whereas the natural and normal effect of literary works is to produce strong subjective modifications in their readers. Our whole method', he insists, 'must therefore be applied so as to rectify our knowledge and purge it of subjective elements.'[3]

[1] Brussels, p. 29.   [2] *Histoire littéraire*, p. 230.
[3] Ibid., p. 231.

Here we have a dichotomy of which Lanson is fond.[1] It suggests comparison with the contemporary opposition between the two cultures, except that the opposition underlying Lanson's phrase irrupts within the mind of its author—and nowhere else. It is a false dichotomy and all it reveals is the incompatibility that exists between the intuitive elements in literature and the 'scientific' mode of approach. 'Our whole method', says Lanson elsewhere, 'is constituted in order to separate subjective impressionism from objective knowledge, to set limits to the former, to control and interpret it for the benefit of objective knowledge.' But this simply means that feeling, imagination, sensibility and taste —all the 'natural and normal' responses to literature are to be abjured when the scientific historian takes over. Put absolutely, the suggestion is absurd and Lanson realizes it. For, having excoriated literature, he recovers and the 'petite phrase' of resignation, the uneasy 'ver irréfutable' murmurs: 'Encore faut-il ne pas pousser cette épuration trop loin' . . .[2]

The fight, we see, is not as straight as it looked. It involves a rearguard action as well as a frontal attack. Lanson wishes to impose a strict methodical discipline on the floating mass of impressionistic teaching into which he finds modern literary studies have sunk. With this predicament the reformer feels he must take a strong line. But the difficulties do not come from the external situation alone or from the laxities and self-indulgences of the 'spécialistes de la légèreté'. Greater difficulties arise from the nature of literature itself. As an intelligent member of a nation which, above all other nations, *se pique de goût*, Lanson has frequently to admit the priority, or at least the validity, of the subjective reaction. Such admissions, as we have seen, crop up incongruously as

[1] Cf. the quotation on p. 35 supra and the Brussels lecture, p. 30.
[2] *Histoire littéraire*, p. 231.

afterthoughts or reservations, pulling against the main thrust of his argument. At such times it is difficult not to feel that he is merely paying lip-service to the claims of taste.

Let us look at some of the effects of Lanson's teaching and example. 'We cannot experiment', he told his Brussels audience, 'We can only observe facts. . . . Each fact is unique of its kind, not by accident but in essence: this is what makes the difference between the literary text and the document in the archive. Everywhere else, even in history, one can apply oneself to the general and leave out the individual differences. But we, even when we seek the general, must retain these differences: otherwise we confuse ourselves in relation to literary history and philosophy. Is it possible for us to take from Racine only what he has in common with Pradon and Quinault? Or to look only at what he bequeathed to Campistron? No: if Racine interests us so much, it is because he is Racine and because of what is only in Racine.'

This was the usual line of attack on Taine, whose system was accused of being incapable of distinguishing between the plays of Pierre Corneille and those of his brother, Thomas. But the same criticism is applicable to Lanson's general attitude and has been applied, *mutatis mutandis*, to the work of his successor. In his *Histoire de la Littérature française classique* (indispensable for the study of the great epoch), Daniel Mornet dealt with the plays of Racine and attempted to assimilate much in them to what he had found elsewhere in the dramatic literature of the time. As one element or attribute after another is derived from, or dissolved back into, 'what we have seen before', the reader may well begin to wonder how much initiative the scholar is going to leave to the playwright. When at last the time comes to discriminate, all we hear by way of differentiation is: 'Racine est poète.' The stop is full.

The distinction drawn between the 'unique fact' in literature and other kinds of fact is no doubt valid. But it is difficult to see that this distinction has been respected in much of the work of the Lansonian school. The facts they have extracted from literature have been too much like common facts. What uniqueness they may have possessed has been effaced in a vast effort to discover, not the particular, but the similar, the comparable, the general, the prototype, the model or the source. And the unprofitable quest for 'influences', pursued as explicit parallels and rehashed according to what I will call the 'ingredient recipe' has corrupted the minds of young learners with the complacent superstition that nothing can be new in literature or the arts. What reader of Lanson's History can forget how conveniently, 'L'ennui, la mélancolie, tout le vague de l'âme de Chateaubriand, séparé de sa puissance pittoresque, formera le courant lamartinien'? Or again how readily, 'Sa tristesse pessimiste, séparée du sentiment chrétien, se retrouvera dans Vigny'? But for the substitution of illustrious names in the place of illustrious victuals, a Briton of Victorian origin like myself might think he was reading a French version of Mrs Beeton.

'Many works are no doubt dead', Lanson admits. 'But the masterpieces are always there, not like documents stored in archives in the fossil state, but like the pictures of Rubens and Rembrandt, active and alive.'[1] Once again embarrassment seizes the present writer as he recalls how, many years ago, he deserted the Faculté des Lettres at the Sorbonne and turned to that of the Fine Arts in order to hear Focillon and Schneider strike a personal note as they pointed to features in the masterpieces reproduced before us. Their lectures on the history of art he found so inspiring a relief that, in an act of folly for which both divine and academic retribution have

[1] Brussels, p. 2.

so far been withheld, he converted most of his remaining cash (there were no *bourses* for foreigners in those days) into a ticket for Florence, and never was truancy more rewarding! So far had it been from the truth that the masterpieces were put before us in the 'literature' course, not a single text, verse or extract had been allowed to appear. Laboriously, biographically, bibliographically, we had climbed the family tree, following the lecturer a foot or two a week, when from a low branch clustered with *aïeux*, the truant slipped off, made for the Gare de Lyon and by dawn was watching Spring advance up the Rhône with Dionysian strides, scattering pink, white and gold on every blossoming bough.

Such a reaction as this, I have now reason to believe, was by no means unique. It has become clear in the interval that other members of those apparently attentive audiences of the '20's in the vast Sorbonne amphitheatre were feeling the depressing inadequacy of a concentrated form of literary history, devoid of the nutrition that direct contact with the texts alone can give.

The separation of feeling from knowledge which Lanson recommends as a safeguard to his method has done much to damage the academic study of French literature, at least until recently. It has led to an abuse of intellectual analysis and recondite comment and to a grave underestimate of the claims of sensibility and the imagination—two of the *sine qua non* which Lanson mentions usually to discredit. The literary humanities, the key to all humanistic study, are exposed to the same mischief today—not so openly perhaps but subversively through infiltrations of erudite techniques. Whereas, I would submit, undergraduates should be allowed and encouraged to read with their full attention as persons of flesh and blood, heart and mind, instead of being trained in the manner of scientific observers to look for general laws common to masterpieces which are to be approached as documents. But no! I err. The dogmatic voice strikes up again and curbs my tentative correction: 'Le point de vue historique remet l'élément subjectif à sa place . . . et désintéresse le critique.' *And makes the critic disinterested* . . . The ideal is obviously not what we should call the literary critic, but the impersonal observer. At times the ruthlessness of the attack on the value of personal reactions seems fantastic. When, once again, the ghost of impressionism returns, we are told, as if to make amends, that we must have 'two tastes (*deux goûts*), a personal taste by which we choose our pleasures, the books and the objects to have around us, and an historic taste which serves our studies and which could be defined as "the art of discerning styles".' This is surely another artificial dichotomy, due to the fact that Lanson is attempting the impossible by striving to identify the critical appreciation of literature with the science of history. Not, of course, that the study of literature has no historical side, but that it has many other sides as well; and perhaps the impressionable people who thought it had an essence or a spirit which it shared with the fine arts, but not with the historical sciences, had perceptions which this vigorous scholar and influential teacher strove at times, with a perverse conscientiousness, to ignore.

Let us glance at the conclusion of this extraordinary document, in which the problem of adapting the method of the historical sciences to the literary humanities was discussed, explored—and I should like to think, as a literary discipline—exposed and exploded with a thoroughness, a pertinacity and a partiality that have probably not been equalled during the last half century of academic controversy.

Now that the tremors have subsided and the persistent echoes of the doctrine of method have become indistinct, what, let us ask, did Lanson prescribe as a programme of work? 'Our principal operations,' he says, 'consist in knowing the texts of literature, in comparing them in order to distinguish the individual from the collective and the original from the traditional; in grouping them by genres, schools and movements and in determining the relationship of these groups to the intellectual, moral and social life of the country, and also to the development of the literature and civilization of Europe.'[1] The effort, we see, is a vast, external (I do not say useless) operation, a general collaboration explicitly designed to lead the individual away from concentration on the individual text and its values. 'Enfin,' says Lanson, 'l'histoire littéraire s'achève par l'expression des rapports de la littérature à la vie, où elle rejoint la sociologie.'[2] When in 1922 the disciples and admirers of the master decided to present him with a *Festschrift*, the strongest marks of gratitude were expressed by those who appreciated his contribution to sociological studies.[3]

Right at the end of his long *exposé* Lanson admits, with disarming loyalty, that it may have produced alarm: 'On sera peut-être effrayé du tableau que je viens de faire.' And he asks—not without reason—what length of life would suffice for the job? 'The history of French literature is a collective enterprise,' he declares. 'Let each one bring his well hewn stone.' The image is only too explicit. Even the beginner has to be engaged in hewing stones for the monument of literary history! 'This,' Lanson admits with a gesture of marvellous insouciance, 'won't prevent anyone from reading what he likes for pleasure.'

The chasm, we see again, is complete between reading and studying—a separation which has, I think, been immensely harmful to French studies and which has sprung from the injections of scientific rationalism that cause the humanities

---

[1] *Histoire littéraire*, p. 240.   [2] Ibid., p. 245.
[3] *Mélanges Lanson*, 1922. See especially the contributions of A. Bayet and H. Bourgin.

to languish everywhere today. Perhaps after all Lanson rendered literary studies a great service by unintentionally exposing the malady it has suffered from under the academic dispensations of the last fifty years.

If finally the question were raised, what kind of philosophy underpins this stern line of argument by which the tyro in literary studies is likened to the hewer of a block of stone, it might not at first be easy to guess. But no possibility of doubt could have been left in the minds of their hearers when, on the conference platform at the Musée Pédagogique, Lanson was followed by his brilliant disciple, Gustave Rudler. What they may well have wondered is whether a narrower, more incisive, even more materialistic educational policy could ever have been proposed in France. The argument crystallized into a hard core of Positivism. Rudler's energetic support not only reinforces Lanson's opening remarks;[1] his fervent accents of scientific prophetism are at times indistinguishable from those of a Taine reprieved and resuscitated. The passage translated below is worth attention, both as a period piece and, I suggest, as a warning of the doom awaiting literary studies if they are ultimately dominated by scientific ideas and directives.

History has been reconstituted as a science and geography has followed suit. Philology has crossed the Rhine and become acclimatized in our midst. Under our very eyes, day by day, literary history is discovering or refining its method, extending its domain, reducing the overflowing fantasies of literary criticism. Grammar and the auxiliary sciences of history are being powerfully developed or created. Ethics seeks its foundations in science. Political economy has changed into sociology. On all hands, whether in the study of nature, man, life, the present or the past,

[1] These need not be summarized after our discussion of the Brussels speech.

the characteristic of science is to advance ceaselessly and with increasing precision, in the exact discrimination of facts, in the close scrutiny of reality. While on all hands science strives towards the real, the exact, the true, the fact, can we remain eternally slumped down in the general, the vague, the probable, the abstract idea, cut off from the fact? While the representation of life and reality becomes richer day by day, can we confine ourselves so strictly to the artistic creation of the past which is only a very limited part of life?

But the methods of science, the spirit of science radiate far beyond science itself. They envelop all contemporary activity. Since 1850, with a few interruptions or waverings, the artist aims at enclosing reality more strictly in the work of art. The bank, which studies how to launch a business, the broker who recognizes a good investment, the industrialist ready to risk his capital, the tradesman who methodically tracks down the evasive customer, the politician who studies the repercussion of his new bill on the multitude of tax-payers are specifically in the same attitude of mind as the historian, the geographer, the philologist; their activity in all cases is ruled by the same reasons; they all tend towards the discovery of facts whose causes they seek and whose effects they aim at foreseeing, provoking or preventing; and the success of their contrivances will depend on the closeness of their grasp of truth. Taking everything into account the really superior mind is the one that has the ability to know, group and handle the greatest number of facts and to draw conclusions from them in the most prompt and intelligent manner.

How can we account for such staggering hard-headedness? It should be explained that Rudler is here combating the traditional practice of using the French essay (*la composition française*) as an exercise in literary style and taste. He wants to make essay-writing—just as Lanson tends to make the study of literature—a training in the detection and manipulation of facts. The exercise should bear 'either on sense data furnished at the present time by the observation of the real or on precise data furnished by the scientific study of the past. We must arm ourselves', he continues, 'against abstract ideas, which are our disease. The activity of the pupils must be directed ... towards the conquest of those forms of knowledge that are positive, precise, visible and tangible ...'

On the factual aspect of education Rudler and Lanson hammer away with an emphasis almost as loud as that of Dickens's school-master, Mr Gradgrind. One can appreciate the force of the reaction from the dilettantism associated with 'cette sorte de sensibilité qu'on appelle la délicatesse littéraire' (a phrase which provoked 'laughter and applause' in Rudler's audience). But the ideal of educating the young *lycéen* on the analogy of brokers and businessmen seems more than a little odd. And since the model is the historian, how many historians, one wonders, would be flattered to hear that they sought and weighed up facts in the way politicians calculate the reactions of tax-payers? With such ideals proposed for young learners and their teachers to follow, is it surprising that 'literary delicacy' was presented as an object of derision?

Such are some of the defects attendant upon a premature importation of scientific notions, attitudes and methods into a field of studies where their use, if and when applicable, should be cautiously adapted.

To lay emphasis on 'facts' to be sought in literature and treated as ultimates seems now so strange a conception even of the scientific task that one wonders whether at any time serious scientists could have accepted it as valid. In any case the conception of science from which it was roughly derived is one that is now completely out of date. It was the science of exact measurements and of 'billiard-ball' atoms regarded as the ultimate facts of the universe. Scientists have not of course ceased to measure. But the recent analysis of the atom has blown the hard-fact theory into fine strontium-laden dust and replaced the dogmatic with the hypothetical. Contemporary science has superannuated the whole basis of assumptions on which these deterministic scholars built. We have moved far from the arrogance of late nineteenth-century scientific rationalism and are being swept into the vaster possibilities and uncertainties of the Nuclear Age. Our conception of the modern humanities must wake up to a world of unprecedented change which has already driven progress through the clown-hoops of 'facts', and which may at any time drive humanity clean off the map of conscious existence. That would be a scientific fact of considerable magnitude—positively a bit of very big business—if anyone were left to profit by it.

One last remark of Lanson's has a pathetic relevance here: his strange belief that historians of literature will help to preserve the peace! Since the scientific history of literature must exhibit no partiality, he was led to the conclusion that 'la dogmatique, fantaisiste ou passionnée, divise: l'histoire littéraire réunit'. This sentiment is expressed at the end both of the long article on *l'Histoire littéraire* and of the speech on *l'Esprit scientifique*. Yet each of these is the utterance of a man who could wax dogmatic and even fanatical in his recommendation of method. As for the power of the history of literature to unite men, the account of what happened at the Conference with the *professeurs de lycée* hardly bears this out. The imposition of a régime that could 'terrify' his hearers might produce peace—the *rigor mortis* of a modern dictatorship. But let us take the remark seriously and ask two broad questions. How far can a conception of literary history which shows no interest in ethical or spiritual values, or in any values at all except those of method, be expected to contribute to the solution of the world's problem of disunity?

Does the society which Lanson left in 1934 look as if even the aftermath of its dissensions is likely to dissolve to the harmonious *roucoulements* of those doves of peace, the scientific historians of literature?

Able and devoted scholars as the Lansonians were, they lacked one saving grace—a grain of humour.

IV

MODERN HUMANITIES IN THE TECHNOLOGICAL AGE
WITH REFERENCE TO THE STUDY OF FRENCH[1]

'Modern Studies need an ideal such as inspired the highest classical studies'—*Modern Languages*, H.M.S.O., 1936.

I FEEL the need to start off with an explanation. What I am going to put before you is a case, a thesis, critical to some extent but also, I hope, suggestive—a thesis which, in the absence of organized thought about universities and their purposes in our time, cannot be other than subjective. I shall try to be frank: what I have to say may even sound dogmatic. But it is not intended to be dictatorial. I believe much time is lost in academic discussion through lack of definiteness in presenting cases or in framing criticisms or suggesting improvements. Proposals and reservations are often made with so much deference and hesitancy that nothing clear emerges for debate: caution pulls the punch, and if we are none the worse, we are none the wiser.

But now I have to ask myself whether I am capable of being clear—whether to put the case effectively is not beyond the powers of any single individual, no matter how broadly experienced or highly placed. The university effort of our time is too fissiparous, too split up into divergent specialisms, for anyone to pronounce in any but the most vague and

[1] From a paper read at the meeting of the Association of Heads of French Departments on 25 March 1957.

general terms on all its varieties of action and diversities of aim, or to attempt to evaluate its disparate achievements. To many of us it must have occurred at one time or another to ask where all this ramifying activity is leading, and what is its end? But good sense persuades the individual that he cannot hope to stand in the midst of so many centrifugal movements and lasso one runaway horse after another with an extended question mark. Even if each horse turned out to be a gift horse and our critic could inspect its teeth, what adjudicator would be able to read all the signs aright and estimate ends many of which, our leading scientists tell us, are only hypothetical after all?

It is not within my terms of reference to review the total activities of our Universities, but rather to consider the nature and purpose of an Honours degree in one subject. I do not, however, feel that this question can be discussed to much effect without attempting to relate it to the wider issue of an Honours degree in Arts, or more pertinently to the problem of humane studies in a time like ours when, as wise men outside the pale keep warning us, universities are helping to stockpile immense quantities of power, but are disseminating all too little enlightenment on how to use it for beneficent purposes.

The predicament of the Arts faculty, which may soon be acutely felt in certain departments, is due, I suggest, to the inadequacy of its organization to maintain the effective balance of university commitments in a technological age. I really am afraid that the majority of active Arts people are not sufficiently aware of, or are curiously silent about, the landslide in dominant studies that is fast gathering way. Arts is ceasing, has in fact since the last war ceased, to be the dominant faculty. It has been deluded by a numerical superiority which is already on the wane. This change is the result of gradual processes in the development of specialization which had begun long before the 'frenzied' acceleration we are now witnessing in the advance of physics and technology. It had been coming, at first surreptitiously, since the spread of the modern universities, since, that is, the middle of the nineteenth century. But the definition of a growing and complex institution or society, like a modern university, is disclosed, not in its origins, but in its development and, I repeat, we Arts people seem in danger of ignoring the fact that the purpose of the modern university movement is being characteristically, though not yet exclusively, identified with the advancement of Science.

If anyone should doubt the validity of this view, let him turn to a recent and objective account of the history of *Civic Universities* by Professor W. H. G. Armytage of Sheffield. Such at any rate is the impression I derived from Professor Armytage's book, and I noticed that another reviewer, with much better rights to assess it than I have, accounted for its drift in the same sense. In the fully equipped scientific university of the future, subjects like our own may find only the kind of niche given to a box of secondary tools—the 'tools of language', as the Americans call them.

It seems obvious that we are only at the beginning of a phase of rapid, and perhaps recklessly unbalanced, expansion, when pure Arts subjects will have to fight hard to retain their position of repute and to maintain their specific and already grievously underrated values. I much wish time permitted me to refer to some of the determined and even violent attacks on the humanities—at least on the *classical* humanities—that have recently been made. But much more serious than the outbursts of active opposition is the attitude of supercilious indifference, linked with an astonishing confidence not only that Science can perform scientific miracles, but that the scientist can do the Arts man's job more effectively than he does it himself; he will even tackle a job like the general problem of morals which few Arts men would admit was within their province.

I am far from being a pessimist. In the dethronement of the ancient classics one may take no kind of pleasure; but one cannot help seeing an opportunity for the *modern* humanities to restore the balance of studies. But will they? The question I want to raise is: Are not the modern humanities—exposed as they find themselves to attacks from without—in worse danger of being undermined *from within* by the sciences of erudition and the techniques of modern research?

The three years' limit of the undergraduate's academic life means that only a taste of good things can be given him. Woe to the profession that filled in that brief space with exacting but impracticable exercises derived from the armoury of research routine, whilst it gave the student no sense at all of the greatness of the subject, forgetting that it is precisely the virtue of many humane subjects that they can be approached without an elaborate technical apparatus. The lessons of a great piece of literature should, for instance, be assimilable at a certain level of effective comprehension by any young person considered fit to be admitted to a faculty of Arts. But a department which handles texts would not be rising to the height of its responsibility toward its younger members if none of its experts attempted to present a great text in terms of its intrinsic values or implications.

Ultimately all depends on the quality of what the student learns for life, not on the quantity of things that are being brought to his notice. We plan ambitiously, but we often seem to forget that the vast majority of students work under a three years' sentence which automatically curtails the effect of many of our best laid schemes and leaves but scraps and smatterings (as Newman predicted) to be salvaged by a stretch of memory from the contemporary fragmentation of studies. In these days of excessive specialization we tend to forget the inevitable: the reputation of a university must in the long run depend on what its *alumni* take away with them and on what they think of it—or whether they think of it at all—afterwards. Sir Walter Moberly was scoffed at for recommending that the university should give every student a philosophy of life. What I suggest is that much of our teaching does not introduce our students to a sufficient number of significant ideas to be ruminated on and built into a personal philosophy of any kind.

To illustrate this point take the idea of Liberty. Some time ago British students, along with many others in western universities, were demonstrating on behalf of Hungary. I suggested to one or two senior academics that probably not more than 20 per cent of the demonstrators had had the chance to learn the meaning of Liberty as a University should expound the idea. My interlocutors were surprised by my assertion, but none could completely refute it. After some argument, however, I felt that my statement would be stronger if in it the proportion of those who could possibly hear a competent treatment of an aspect of the problem of Liberty were raised to 30 per cent.

I then pointed to the enormous number of student lives sacrificed to the idea within the last fifty years. I instanced the terrible loss of young Frenchmen in the first World War. Liberty of determination in the broadest sense was what these students thought they were defending, yet the vast majority of those who fell or were mutilated suffered for freedom instinctively and spontaneously, having probably received little or no intimation of the difficulties involved in the problem of Liberty, individual and national—'that most exhilarating and most precarious of political ideals' as Mr Maurice Cranston has said.[1]

The discussion of Liberty leads naturally to that of Tolera-

[1] *The Listener*, 10 January 1957.

tion, the gift of three centuries of noble effort in France and England which has been trampled in blood and dust by the tyrants of our own—*this* century which was to have been the 'halcyon' age of Science, predicted by the first Secretary of the Royal Society, Thomas Sprat, but in whose most spectacular achievements so far, he could only have seen a hideous caricature of his hopes.

Inquiries about most of the big ideas basic to civilization might receive equally dusty answers so far as the discussion of them goes with the majority of present-day undergraduates. But my argument is not concerned to suggest that more arrangements should be made for the general education of the student. I do not disapprove of courses in general education. But it is illogical to point to them when the question is asked: How many of the great ideas are conveyed through the regular teaching of undergraduates? Nor is the question rhetorical. The scientists at least don't appear to think so; and it is *they* who have the only clear answer that the contemporary university can claim to give.

For there is certainly one idea that no student of Science is likely to miss and which is repeated on all hands in an exclusive and dogmatic form. It is that the university exists solely to discover knowledge and that new knowledge is truth. I hesitate to suggest that any eminent scientist is responsible for this popular version of the motto, but the assumption is made in high places and the motto is proposed and apparently accepted as the *raison d'être* for the whole university effort without distinction of aim.

Now the discovery of new knowledge seems properly enough to be the object of the pioneering advance of Science; but the leap into metaphysics with which its advertisement is accompanied needs a sharp examination of the kind the late Professor Susan Stebbing used to give to the metaphysical flights of the scientists of her day.

I am not myself able to tackle the ambiguities in the phrase. But I will venture to say that even if, at the dictation of the scientists, we all accept the quest of knowledge that leads to truth as our motto, we need surely not agree that every department seeks knowledge along the same lines or by the same means. Indeed there are many kinds of knowledge, and what truths it is given us to perceive in universities that preclude the category of the spiritual cannot be other than relative truths. Otherwise, how could there be any differentiation between Arts and Science?

With this question we seem to be brought back to the popular distinction that Arts seek knowledge and truth about the human, Science seeks the same about the inhuman. But no sooner is this distinction registered than it is jeopardized by the realization that several popular subjects stand astride both faculties. Note that these subjects are on the increase, and are attracting more students and more admirers. Lord Adrian, when President of the British Association, said that no antidote to the bomb was likely to be found in atomic science; the only hope was in the social sciences. The report of his speech omitted all reference to Arts. These blended subjects may mediate between Arts and Science, but they advance at the expense of the humanities.

The humanities are discredited and rejected. They are being attacked openly *de front*, while those who should defend them remain silent and inactive; and they are being undermined from within. The most insidious undermining movement operates through a more or less unconscious abuse of erudition and of the techniques of rational scholarship in the teaching of humane subjects. Research is at once the flower and the virus of Arts. Under the impetus of powerful movements like the history of literature and the history of language, a ponderous wedge has been thrust between the undergraduate and the great texts of humanism;

and undergraduates by their thousands have been directed to regard such texts as examples for scholarly comment and technical observation rather than as the terminal objects they should be studying for the good that is in them for the reader. (The 'good' I refer to would have to be defined; its definition would be the definition of true humanism.) So, in my student days, the death of Roland could become a number of words to be etymologized and nothing more—at least for the teacher; while later on *Les Fleurs du Mal* has been found to contain so many signs of miscellaneous reading that the student is induced to question the originality of Baudelaire, even before he has read the poems. He can no longer look at the magnificent opening of *La Mort du Loup* without being told by a scholar who has written a book on Vigny *for him* that no huntsman could approach a wolf so closely as Vigny describes his huntsmen as having done. The authority for this piece of honest impertinence is the textbook-maker's brother; you see how the domineering scholar will bring even a member of his family in to refute a mere poet.

I cannot suppress reference to another *petite bête* in a well-known textbook on French Romantic poetry. In the purely impressionistic landscape of Lamartine's *Isolement* a spire is mentioned. Thereupon the commentator steps forward and tells the pupil: 'This poem was probably written at Milly; but there isn't a spire in the landscape around Milly.' I wish the commentator had commented further on the purpose or relevance of this remark. Since realism seems his cue, would it not have been wise to make quite sure that the poem was written at Milly and that Lamartine was looking out of the window when he wrote it, and that he held a goose quill and not the swan's feather which Mallarmé *probably* used when he wrote that famous sonnet which commemorates the thwarted aspirations of ten thousand undergraduates in 'les vols qui n'ont pas fui'?

Yet these, alas, are only pin-points of the glaciers of aggressive erudition on which, if we are not on the sharpest look-out, the teaching of French literature—the unique modern classical literature—will founder, and the gulf between a self-centred and self-defeating scholarship and the true critical approach to a living literature will widen until Science steps in and claims the lot. Do not forget Taine's warning: 'Elle approche enfin, et elle approche de l'homme. Elle a dépassé le monde visible et palpable des arbres, des pierres, des plantes, où dédaigneusement on la confinait. C'est à l'âme qu'elle se prend. . . .'

It is high time that I came to our specific subject. Reverting to the basic ideas, some at least of which should, I suggested, be seriously presented and discussed in the course of a student's education in Arts, let me remind you that they occur in at least two common forms available for study. They are expressed either as abstractions in philosophy, ethics or dogma—and this I will call *direct* expression, i.e. the ideas occur as concepts. Or they may be presented indirectly in concrete and vital forms as in literature and the fine arts. Here the idea may never be expressed as such: it is more likely to be symbolized dramatically, and imaginatively treated as lived or acted. And note that what I have called an 'idea', so far from being a concept, may be a fundamental attitude discussed through a conflict of motives exhibited in the speech and gestures of *dramatis personae*.

Now I hasten to say, before the hearts of many distinguished teachers of literature sink at the prospect, that I am not suggesting that literature should be taught solely for the discussion of what ideas it may contain. I do, however, suggest that the greater forms of literature offer the most inclusive presentation of the ethos, attitudes, standards, motives, significant myths and psychological types that characterize a great civilization, and that it is essentially literature of this kind that constitutes the ready-to-hand, invaluable stuff of humanistic studies. But—and this is the main distinction I have striven to make from the beginning—in order to present such literature in the rich and nourishing sense as 'classics', one must lead students to its appreciation in terms of its essential greatness.

On the contrary, as is now and then forcibly pointed out, what has so often been done is to divert the students' attention into channels of biography, influence, versification, grammar—for which the text becomes the illustration of an extraneous specialism or an exercise in technique. This is not humanism. Forgive the caricature: 'l'érudition n'est pas un humanisme!' And the sad truth is, I'm afraid, that the technical approach, however well conducted—*les techniques de la critique*—may count for little or nothing to the graduate when he has left the department—unless indeed the graduate becomes a researcher, when it may recover its practical value as an initiation.

But have we often asked ourselves what percentage of our students *do* become researchers and whether many more of them are likely to do so in the great era of technological research which has just opened? Are we in Arts likely to keep abreast of that torrent of productivity? Who is going to appreciate *our* quota as the spaceships flit up the light-years and return with power enough to blast all the planets they pass into stars? We are obviously called to another kind of task—to help the young left on earth to appreciate why great literature is still great and why it is humane. And that in its way is a task as exacting and exciting as pin-pointing human targets with bigger and brighter bombs. Only, this task of ours will be muffed if the great themes become submerged under the research interests of the teacher. This is what T. R. Glover of Cambridge said about the same danger over twenty years ago: 'Too much of our Classical work is open to the reproach that we sacrifice end to means and that, in our Colleges, forgetful of man and citizen, oblivious of life, we devote ourselves to training specialists who restore texts and pursue minutiæ and forget to read great literature.'[1]

My first suggestion, then—to be practical at last—is a borrowed one, but it is worth repeating: That Honours in our subject should be conceived as a type of humane study, a course in *modern* humanities, not excluding the medieval, which also should be presented as a humanistic course and not as what a serious philologist once described it as being: a course in antiquarianism (his reference was not to French). The choice should lie in the greatest examples, and these should be studied for the most human lessons they contain. By 'lessons' I mean the real significance of the piece of literature as critical appreciation seizes and evaluates it. Analysis there will have to be; but the best presentation will pass beyond analytical comment to an awareness and appraisal of the synthesis of values that a great work is. The whole approach will of course be based on sound scholarship, if not necessarily on the very latest research. But this should not be obtrusive, and normally the research will have been done by the teacher or by someone other than the undergraduate. The student should, of course, be led to appreciate the modes of scholarly approach, but his education must not stop there or consist in too many exercises in technique and method. He should be allowed to see Roland die as he dies in the epic. The teacher may comment if he has anything to say *à la hauteur*, but he should remember that he is annotating the sublime. The great moments in literature should be indicated, but are better left to the direct apprehension of the reader, provided of course that he *can* read the text. But while he is trying to learn the language of the

[1] T. R. Glover, *Purpose in Classical Studies* (address delivered to the Classical Association, 1938).

Chanson, don't please encumber him with the language of the Oaths of Strasbourg, the language of Villon, the language of Rabelais, the language of Racine, the language of Mallarmé and the language of André Breton. In plain language, that would be an *embarras de richesses* which would break the back of the *bête de somme*: let him go to paradise with Francis Jammes and the asses, even if we don't go there ourselves! Or to quote Glover again in all seriousness: 'It is a poor literature that is not a better training for a man than the acquisition of the means of reading it.'

May I indulge just two more suggestions, dear to my heart and not, I think, remote from the present discussion?

French is a more abstract language than ours and the French brain superior at manipulating abstractions. I believe that the biggest intellectual defect of the British student (although it might be safer to exclude the North British student from this sweeping statement) is his relatively poor grasp and feeble use of abstract ideas. The superb facility the French have for expressing and systematizing ideas makes them ideal teachers of the British intelligentsia, who share this, at least, with their Latin neighbours that their ideal schemes rest finally on earth, in contact with men and things, realities and artifacts—as opposed to the Germans who fly their kites so high that they seem to get lifted off their feet, and who when they philosophize aloud leave us wondering what we have been listening to. Most Britishers of my age were brought up to think of Germany as the great manufactory of modern thought, and of France as the world's intellectual clearing-house, where the volumes of Teutonic lucubration could be condensed, winnowed and turned into brilliant monographs that anyone could read, provided he knew a little French and was moderately intelligent.

Now do we make enough of this important side of French expression? I have often asked myself whether we could contrive to put more specimens of French thought into our syllabuses. The literature of *haute vulgarisation* would, I admit, be a secondary category compared with the creative and imaginative genres; but we cannot be logical throughout our prescriptions. Considering my own inability to read abstract philosophy at source, I could not recommend that we draw much from that category—apart from Descartes. Within the limits of my comprehension and experience as a teacher I suggest that, while a selection of Montaigne's essays meets the case admirably, more modern examples should be found. Toynbee has recently shown what provocative contrasts can be evoked from a choice of passages on toleration from Pierre Bayle. A careful selection of Valéry's essays (not necessarily one of his own *Variété* series) would be attractive; and I have sometimes thought that Julien Benda's *Trahison des Clercs* might stimulate argument on things that matter to young intellectuals today.

Notice, on the other hand, that modern French poetry (the teaching craze of the post-war period) hardly meets the requirement—although modern poetic theory might qualify. Like all forms of poetry since the beginning of Romanticism, French poetry of the last hundred years has become increasingly *imaged*—that means concrete in language. Is it not amazing how sensational the poetry of France has become—once the purest efflorescence of the intellectual imagination? Sensations our young people can find in only too great abundance everywhere: what they are starved of is a continuum of intelligible thought.

Such reading as I have suggested would help our students in their efforts to communicate with students abroad, who habitually employ more mature modes of expression; it might supply ideas more solidly conducive to a genuine *entente* than friendships formed on social gossip and warmhearted agreements about items on a menu.

Our undergraduates appear to be active-minded and well disposed to work—though I note there are doubts about the seriousness of many of them in some parts of the profession. As *thinkers*, however, all but the best of them are really too young for their age. I admit at once that many of them grow up rapidly in their third year. But how is it that our curriculum does not help them to mature earlier?

Let us pause and ask ourselves what students of a foreign language and literature are doing most of their time? Whether on their own initiative or in obedience to regulations, many of them are multiplying juvenile initiations and picking up scraps of the vocabulary and grammar of two or three languages at once, while they may be wrestling with (or merely memorizing) different phases of the main language of their course; in addition, on a more intellectual level, they will be involved in tackling problems of the nature and history of language along diverse specialized lines.

To show what I mean, let us turn in thought to Professor R. C. Knight's very useful book of *Advice*. Here are displayed with (so far as I can judge) scrupulous fidelity to every aspect of our subject, several forms of language study, several specialisms, all presented without preference or bias and with helpful explanations of exercises in which I once engaged like M. Jourdain, without knowing what I was up to. They include, not only the imposing categories of pre-war days—'Historical Philology: Phonology, Morphology, Syntax, Semantics', but also—as Professor Knight's collaborator, Dr George, warns the reader—'you may be offered lectures on other aspects of French linguistics: on stylistics, on the structure of present-day French, on the work of linguistic geographers and so on. So many different courses are possible that we cannot hope to deal with them individually here. . . .'

To these one must add the cluster of practical exercises that constitute Phonetics for the student. And even now the procession—which to the apprehensive freshman might appear somewhat like the approach of the doctors in *Le Malade Imaginaire*—is not complete; for here, towering above the spate of specialisms, comes the Don Quixote of language exercises since the Renaissance—Prose Composition on the Latin model—accompanied by Sancho Panza, the *version*, bringing up the rear on a sadly neglected nag. . . .

But now I must pull myself up and admit the reservation you must have been making from the beginning of this enumeration. No student does all these things at once and few perhaps sample them all in the course of three years. True. The point I want to make is not a provocative one. Some of these initiations and exercises are necessary and, in any case, the language must be learnt in its modern form; but I don't see how it can be denied that such occupations mount up to a formidable total and that they limit the time at the disposal of the undergraduate and of the department for the study of *litterae humaniores*. In other words the more we specialize the more our subject splits into curricula of divergent prescriptions.

And this brings me to my very last suggestion, which I will put into the form of a question. In view of the generosity we exhibit in crowding the undergraduate's programme with things, all of which may be intrinsically good, I ask: Is it not possible that our subject, in conception and in application, is planned and run on a scale at once too extensive and too inclusive to produce the maximum of practical effectiveness?

I have often wondered whether one or both of the following schemes might be worth trying in place of the present arrangement of studies, assembled from a very wide field of choice. First, that departments should differentiate themselves more than they do by predominant interests. Such interests would be above the level of skills (like language-teaching), but not too specialized for effective use with undergraduates. Some departments might show a preference for linguistics; others might favour history and institutions; others would be notable for textual criticism; and there might be more chronological differentiation in the study of literature and art. Students in one department who were discovered to have strong aptitudes for the major specialism of another would be seconded to that department, and there would be redistribution of such students at or before the end of the second year.

I foresee many objections to such a scheme, which would normally apply only to undergraduates of decided tastes and abilities, but which might have for them some of the magnetic attraction that famous university courses and teachers had in earlier periods. (And let me ask in parenthesis why that kind of attraction has disappeared so largely from Arts?)

Yet the experiment which I like to think might have more chance of adoption would be to attempt a major subdivision of studies chronologically differentiated into (i) Medieval and Renaissance and (ii) Renaissance and Modern. One can well imagine schools of medieval studies of great scholarly value and deep humanistic interest, developed through a combination of different departments in the same centre having similar interests. And this brings me to one final point which is not original and therefore permits a compliment to be offered to those of you who have already succeeded in uniting with other departments to produce combined Honours schemes of four years' duration. Such schemes hold out perhaps the brightest hopes for humane studies in conformity with the often-cited advice of Flexner, that university courses should be both 'broad and deep'.

No great civilization has subsisted without some form of

mature education relevant, not only to the practical needs of that civilization but, even more, to the inculcation of its highest ideals. Acknowledging that you have illustrated our profession by the production of much scholarship, competent, useful and sometimes brilliant, for your next task I should like to submit a formula from the well known essay of Ortega y Gasset and to recommend a 'theory of the University' or, in terms of our subject, a well-meditated plan of campaign on behalf of the modern humanities.

In the *Times Educational Supplement* for 23 March 1957 there was a *Comment* too pertinent to miss. It read:

M. Pierre Mendès-France said that applied and fundamental research was a matter of life or death for France. The Minister of Education solemnly vowed to lure more students into modern courses and to find the teachers for them. But if France is wise she will still make sure, as she has done until now, that every educated Frenchmen, scientist or not, is deeply grounded in that humane and European culture of which she is, in a special sense, the guardian.

There is a hint for us here. While our Science colleagues split atoms and cruise along the outer edges of space, let us apply the example France has set us and attempt to preserve the type *human* on one speck of dust in the apparently endless reaches of the inhuman universe.

V

PROFICIENCY IN MODERN LANGUAGES[1]

THIS chapter attempts to raise explicitly an aspect of the problem of modern studies which received too little attention in the past, but has now become recognized as a requirement of wide and pressing importance. It is, moreover, the *sine qua non* for almost all work involving foreign media, and must in particular affect or determine the degree of success to be achieved in dealing with whatever content or objective characterizes such courses as are provided for senior pupils and undergraduates. I refer to the degree of proficiency attained in the use of a language in its modern or contemporary forms. What can be done with or through a language obviously depends upon how well the language is known. The paradox of the present situation is this. We are liberally contriving opportunities (or compulsions) for thousands of young people to learn languages without our being equally concerned to ascertain whether the languages are actually learned or not by anything like the whole of this multitude of intended beneficiaries. Most people, I think, who have watched the examination machine at work temper their respect for the rigour of its operations with doubts about the inerrancy of its discriminations. Many at least would agree that public examination results are by no means

[1] From an article published in *Universities Quarterly*, May 1949. See also articles by Professors Peacock and Entwistle in *Universities Quarterly*, February and August 1948.

invariably reliable as exact records of proficiency in languages.

To avoid misunderstandings, certain reservations to the implication of these remarks must at once be admitted. They are not, for example, intended to apply to the very best pupils at the Advanced stage, still less to the most brilliant of Honours students. It is a fact, however, that even within Honours groups, more or less serious degrees of unproficiency are prevalent below the top level; while from the Honours grade downwards the work of language students, not to mention that of pupils at school, can show grave inequalities of standard. Creditable achievements occur at all stages. But it is undeniable that language work can sink through gradations of dubious competence to depths of incompetence involving hundreds of young people annually in aimless and fruitless dissipation of energies which could have been directed to more useful objectives, free from the deterrent of having to acquire a medium.

After thirty years' experience in most kinds of examining, thinking exclusively for the moment of the state of the language (with acknowledgements of progress made in many quarters), I confess to having often felt puzzled to know what is really the object of the large-scale study of French in this country. Or to start with a more rudimentary form of question: Why are so many children taught foreign languages? In putting the matter in this blunt way, I am as anxious not to single out the schools for disproportionate blame as I am eager to admit the rapid advance that can be made by beginners, if well taught—a rate of progress oftentimes deceptive, if judged by later achievements.

To discover an answer to the foregoing question, I have opened books like the *Memorandum on the Teaching of Modern Languages*, issued by the Incorporated Association of Assistant Masters in Secondary Schools, and turning to the first chapter on the Aims of Language Teaching, I have relapsed into vagueness and doubt. Take this curiously worded passage: 'What will he (the Modern Language teacher) seek to give his pupils, beyond helping in their general development, that only the study of a modern language can give?—It is not easy to give a clear and definite answer. The Committee found in the course of its work that most terms used generally, and by its own members, in defining aims were understood in several varying senses. . . .' It is typical, I fear, of the indefinite nature of educational operations that the question 'Why learn a modern language?' dissolves into an admission of the terminological confusions that arise in attempting to frame the question itself. From books I turned to persons and interrogated among others a former high official of the Board of Education, who although not a modern language expert, was admirably conversant with French and interested in the fortunes of that language in this country. He would hear nothing of treating language learning as a means of training the faculties and insisted that a language should be taught for use.

What degree of proficiency is implied in teaching a language for use? In other words, what do we mean by 'proficiency'? This word, like most of those used in contemporary education, does not stand for a stable or objective standard or even for a clear and distinct idea. It is obvious that there are academic standards of *relative* proficiency which differ very considerably from that absolute which Dr H. E. Palmer appears to have had in mind when he defined the object of language teaching as to enable the foreign pupil to speak like a native, read like a native, and write like a native. Here Dr Palmer is doubtless thinking of ideals to be kept in view. He would probably agree with most of us that in practice there are many different grades of proficiency appropriate to different stages of the pupil-student's career.

What I am concerned to ask is, how much language does a pupil or student know when he has finished his course? Or more precisely, how nearly do academic standards correspond to useful degrees of real proficiency?

Let us attempt to visualize this situation. Who has not at the close of a session's various examining, especially if it has included much school work, had the sensation of landing from a choppy sea, an ocean of tossing results, crossed by a few high waves arriving at odd intervals to lift his bark from the slough of despond? Who has not realized as he shakes off the brine, that great numbers of those who are left in the slough will remain there for ever, for what hopes of rescue they have from institutional language teaching? And who has not asked, what does it all amount to for the foundered? The Harvard report of 1945, *General Education in a Free Society*, frankly admitted that low-grade language instruction is justifiable only as ancillary to the learning of the mother-tongue. Well, after nearly a century of French and German teaching, what had the Norwood Report to say about the state of English?

At the university level there can never have been a time when so many undergraduates as at present had so insecure a grasp of the languages they had begun to learn four or five years before leaving school. Grammar has become nebulous —or is it that too many 'grammars' are being taught at once? As for Phonetics they flourish in some quarters and seem to have become extinct in others. Let me repeat: the plight of hundreds of undergraduates is not due solely to insufficient preparation at school. However well they do their work, the schools can hardly be expected to transform the majority of their numerous pupils into so many good linguists. A large part of the difficulty lies in the disproportion between the language-teaching resources of university departments and the size of their classes which can dwarf the largest class the schools justly complain of. The departments, however talented their staff, however brilliant their record, are not equipped to engage in the task of bringing the majority of their students to a high level of practical competence in the all-round command of foreign tongues. Such an objective would require more teachers, tutors, coaches and crammers, and far more time devoted to the language in its modern form, than any department could possibly afford, having regard to the intellectual content of the subject and of other subjects in which the undergraduate may be interested. The contrast between our leisurely modes of language teaching, modelled largely on Latin, and the methods adopted by Army Language Schools would doubtless be instructive. But for the university to exchange one model for another would be to risk turning the departments into commercial language schools; and that of course no one wants.

If, adding to the numbers of students of French those in other popular language departments, one pauses to realize what proportion of a Faculty of Arts are 'doing languages', the spectacle of frustration takes on dimensions any cool estimate of which might seem an exaggeration to the common reader. I will content myself with a couple of questions, one general, one specific. First, in the general economy of the national education, having in mind the schemes of study, curricula and equipment now in vogue, has not saturation point in the recruitment for languages already been reached? Or, more simply, is not the educational system of this country carrying more language-learners than it can effectively provide for on present resources—resources which on the mechanical side may often seem fantastically inadequate? How many foreign language departments, apart from the few that can draw upon a practical phonetics section, are not still running on blackboard-and-chalk lines in a world of television, super-cinemas and split atoms? What I really want to get at is this: judged from the standpoint of values, educational, cultural and practical, have languages (apart always from the mother tongue) a right to preferential treatment? Given limited block grants in perpetuity, should further expansions, in languages, for instance, take preference over Social Studies?[1]

My second question is, what can be done now to husband resources at the university level? Neither question can be dealt with adequately here. But I will attempt to answer the latter in so far as it applies to one aspect of the *modus operandi*, namely to the condition of students in their first year or at the junior grades.

Much error and waste in Arts practice have been due to the false assumption that the 'Intermediate' or first-year stage in languages invariably corresponds to a useful degree of proficiency. This has led to the imposition of single-year end-stopped courses (usually in Latin and/or modern languages) of a grade too low to yield satisfactory results in all but a small percentage of cases. Such compulsions, it must be admitted, are now being modified or abandoned in certain quarters. Yet in most Arts schemes the regulations still constrain, canalize or inveigle students, proficient or otherwise, into taking courses of this kind either as a count towards the total of degree requirements or as ancillary to other courses. The latter might be thought the more serious claim. Ancillary accomplishments are no doubt desirable. But provision for them should be made outside the scheme of studies for the degree. It is an odd recommendation of a university course to call it a 'tool', as the Americans do, to distinguish this secondary type of utility. Moreover, courses which

[1] I am not assuming that the present *disproportion* of learners as between one foreign language and another is satisfactory. Nor do I demur at the necessity of providing for certain languages not hitherto taught in this country.

prescribe the acquisition of media for one year only are obviously not the most useful for expanding the students' range of knowledge.[1] The more proficient, as everyone knows, kick their heels; as for the others, the pseudo-'Intermediate' becomes a demi-semi-final, leading nowhere beyond itself.

This is how the contrivance works. Out of some hundreds of examination scripts nearly a half may fail to procure the pass-mark of 50 per cent. The resultant holocaust will look like a responsible act on the part of the executioners. But what of the victims themselves, who have lost a year struggling with a subject which most of them may never have wanted to take? Cases of such magnitude are by no means rare. But it is the proportion of the 'lost' I want to draw attention to. The mischief is common in many forms. Suppose, as often happens, a minimum of 25 per cent of Final Pass candidates fail, and that another 25 per cent pass at between 50 per cent and 55 per cent of the marks. Such pass-marks give no guarantee of reliable proficiency on the language side even at the university stage.

This game of rebuilding Babel annually at the expense of hundreds of undergraduates absorbs much of the energy of scores of assistant lecturers, employed in correcting exercises in which gross incompetence only too often triumphs over pathetic efforts to improve—'To the greater Glory of God', as a student of mine persistently wrote above her lamentable exercises! What earthly progress could she hope to make in eight months as member of a large class meeting a remote, if conscientious, teacher three or four times a week? 'Babel'

[1] It will of course be claimed that all language Intermediate courses carry some useful 'content'. True; but why not reduce the less profitable side to a minimum, show a sign of reckless ingenuity: abolish the 'prose' exercise, teach reading alone, and let the students concerned learn more about France and Germany in their own language? They might pick up many things which Honours students have to go abroad for.

indeed is a euphemism for a situation in which a good half of our language students find little or no chance to 'talk' in departments which have difficulty enough in providing oral opportunities for the upper ten. For to rid our centres of illumination of such ephemerae as are directed towards the gleams they can never overtake would but clear the air. We should still be faced with the responsibility of maintaining such standards in the use of the modern tongue as the better students have brought up from their schools—a sufficiently onerous responsibility as yet by no means fully discharged to every student's satisfaction.

One of our wisest minds was reported to have referred to 'the tendency to assume that everyone should be educated rather than that the highest standard of education for the few should be maintained'.[1] With the reservation that a nation of forty-eight millions could be expected to produce 100,000 young people worthy of some kind of university education, I perceive a sense in which the quotation applies to my present argument. It would probably be agreed that the highest justification for teaching a foreign language is that its acquisition provides a key to another national culture and facilitates the comprehension of other modes of life, including the appreciation of alien political attitudes. However desirable it might seem that the majority of one nation should be able to communicate with the majority of another, such an ideal is still so far from practicable that, unless some way is found of teaching and learning languages more quickly and more securely, we may soon see the establishment of artificial media for many urgent, non-cultural purposes. For what is being obscured today by all this 'language-learning business', with its proliferation of certificates gained at low pressure, is the irrefutable fact that to acquire a foreign

[1] Attributed to Mr T. S. Eliot by a reviewer in the *New Statesman and Nation*, 21 June 1947.

tongue thoroughly is a strenuous and difficult job for all but specially gifted or advantaged adepts. Academic methods may be sound and sure; they are undeniably slow to produce results and slower to revise their own technique. I have not been advocating a drastic reduction of the total of language learners. But I should like to suggest: (i) that there be a more equitable and useful balance of learners as between the prominent world languages; (ii) that it might be advisable to concentrate teaching resources upon those pupils and students who show aptitude while the others are diverted to more suitable studies or employments; (iii) that no language department admit students for less than two consecutive years; (iv) that each language-teaching nucleus be strengthened in its establishment and equipped with every appropriate device for promoting all round competence in the majority of its members; (v) that the presentation of language subjects, the relative value of contents and the practical effectiveness of exercises be seriously reconsidered in the light not only of recent discussions but of the observations and implications contained in the Government report on *Modern Studies* of 1926; (vi) that more numerous facilities be provided to enable teachers and learners to sojourn abroad at frequent intervals; and (vii) that lending libraries of foreign books be founded at centres convenient for distribution to teachers outside the few great towns that provide such resources.

PART TWO

COMMENTARIES & DISCUSSIONS

VI

THE FORMAL METHOD ARRAIGNED

Is the accredited mode of *Explication* adequate to the presentation of Modern Poetry?[1]

IN the course of the stimulating attack on the formal method of literary analysis which he delivered as President of the Modern Language Association for 1961,[2] Professor Vinaver made one condition clear, that what he was discussing was not—in his own words—'the usefulness of the method as a form of training in rational analysis, but its suitability for purposes of literary study'. 'My only contention,' he said, 'is that the method of *explication* as traditionally conceived is not, and never could be, the proper means of discovering great poetry and prose.'

I find myself all the more heartily in agreement with this attitude as I have been working along lines of my own which have brought me to a similar conclusion. And having acknowledged Professor Vinaver's lead, I must refer to two other documents which have been of great help to me. One of them has particular interest because it is actually an apologia for the method itself, and is by Gustave Lanson. I want to spend a little time on Lanson's recommendations because I think they hold the key to the deficiencies as well as to the utilities of the method.[3]

---

[1] A paper prepared at the invitation of the East-Yorkshire branch of the Modern Language Association.
[2] See *Modern Languages*, March 1961.
[3] '... il excellait dans l'exercice que notre enseignement considère à

My third *pièce justificative* is a find, a *trouvaille* placed in my hands by some Bangor friends who are as much interested as any of us in the teaching of French literature. This I will keep as a surprise.

Some of you may have come across a small thin book called *Méthodes de l'Histoire littéraire*, which was published in Paris in 1925, under the ægis of the French university teachers of America. It is composed of a selection of Lanson's speeches, and these include one on the French method of literary commentary. It begins in a significant manner. Lanson confesses that an American friend (who must have been someone of importance in the educational hierarchy) had asked him the question: 'Who was the torturer that invented the explication of texts?' Lanson's reply is characteristically prompt and confident. It is a defence of the method that has become widely known as *l'explication française*.

First he accepts with marked complacency the fact that it is an 'artificial' exercise and that pupils must be compelled to confront difficulties in literary studies as they do in all other initiations, including sport. It is clear at once that the study of literary texts is to be a hard training imposed upon the learners 'in order to teach them to read'. Lanson makes a sharp distinction, as we have seen, between reading for pleasure and reading according to the precepts and practice of the methodical initiation.

In his study of Ezra Pound, Mr G. S. Fraser[1] writes: 'A good teacher always tells his pupils that a subject must be dull, there must be a great deal of grind in it, before it becomes interesting.' Lanson hammers away at the grind

---

bon droit son joyau, et qui est "l'explication de textes".' *Allocution d'André François-Poncet* at the celebration of Lanson's centenary, Paris, 1958.

[1] Fraser, *Ezra Pound*, (Oliver and Boyd), p. 16.

but forgets about the 'interest'. He never mentions the possibility of reading with intelligent enjoyment. One cannot resist the feeling that the text is to be used less to teach reading than to 'train the mind', to train it to concentrate, and above all to concentrate according to a certain preordained method. The attention, of course, has to be trained. But the danger with so much of the work prescribed in universities as in the schools today is that we achieve our fixed objectives by making use of texts for ends ulterior to, and sometimes remote from, 'what the texts themselves appear to have been written for'. With Lanson the objective is strictly pedagogical. Listen to the comparison he makes to clinch his argument at this point: 'The primary school teacher,' he says, 'teaches the alphabet; the secondary school teacher teaches how to read literature ...' Lanson's comparisons are forceful but not ingratiating. We shall see in a moment what a contemporary *professeur de lycée* thinks of the method he extolled.

I can best perhaps begin to explain what I find unsatisfactory in Lanson's attitude by considering what *he* thinks is the strongest point in his argument. 'In a word', he says emphatically, 'to read with reflection, to read with understanding, to read not only in order to give oneself strong or multiple impressions, but to acquire a clear, precise and distinct understanding of the texts—all this is something that cannot be done alone: it is something that has to be learnt, and this is the ideal thing that is learnt by the exercise called *l'explication de textes.*'

It would be unreasonable to take exception to the aims of clarity and precision. They are of course basic requirements in teaching and learning. But note the actual phrase that Lanson uses: 'pour acquérir une intelligence *claire, précise* et *distincte.*' Are not the epithets familiar? Two of them were used by Descartes in his famous *Discours.* Lanson is at heart a Cartesian; he deals best with literature of the eighteenth-century type. In 1906 he wrote so good a monograph on Voltaire that it has been re-published, in a revised form, over fifty years later.

The author of the *Discours de la Méthode* is obviously an inspirer of the modern master of method. And here arises a dilemma! I assume we should all agree that the first, and probably the most important, initiation we have to give our pupils and students is good method—order, precision and clarity in the grasp of the subject *and* in what account we expect them to give of it. But what attitude are we to adopt, for example, to the treatment of modern poetry? There, I fear, precision methods *à la* Lanson will not carry us very far. We have to find methods of much greater freedom and of finer adaptability to types of poetry in which, to quote Verlaine, 'l'Indécis au Précis se joint'.

I must now try to show why, and in what sense, the formal method is inadequate to this and similar tasks. To begin, I want to contend that the unsuitability of the method for literary purposes is shown up by Lanson himself. A vigorous rather than a subtle thinker or speaker, he had a weakness for making his propositions sound like absolute decrees or at least for presenting them dogmatically. The fact is, he says, that most people do not know how to read. How many, he asks, can repeat the content exactly and explain its meaning without alteration, without adding anything to it or withdrawing from it? 'Try the experiment, you'll see . . .', he says.

Let us pause to ask in turn, how many of us could satisfy such excruciating tests of memory? Yet how many of us believe, and feel we have good reason to believe, that we can read Baudelaire, for instance, with far more intelligence and appreciation than Lanson showed in his grudging account and misjudgment of one of the most influential, and still much appreciated, poets of the nineteenth century?

At this point in Lanson's discourse there occurs, one must admit, an ingratiating reservation, which reminds one of his reputation for intellectual probity. Having declared his belief that a text has an objective meaning independent of the individual reader's mind and sensibility, he appends in a footnote a disarming afterthought, inspired by reading Proust. This experience leads him to confess that he does not now feel so sure about the 'objective meaning'. The self and the non-self, he perceives, are inseparably blended in all perception and knowledge. '*A relativist conception of the study of the text is, therefore, perfectly possible*' ... This admission does honour to Lanson's scrupulousness. But does it not, at the same time, undermine and invalidate much of his dogmatism? Not long ago Professor Pierre Moreau quoted this footnote in his useful little book, *La Critique littéraire en France*, to show that Lanson submitted himself to a veritable 'examen de conscience' in his last years. And he could have shown that a far more important *volte-face* had happened earlier in Lanson's career, which had transformed him from a genuine literary scholar and critic into a scientific or pseudo-scientific historian of literature with results not free from ambiguity and confusion.

Some of the more serious reservations that he makes to his dogmatic assertions and injunctions look very much like *reversals* of his whole attitude. They seem to give so much away that one wonders how much can be left. 'Even in works where ideas dominate and truth is the essential rather than beauty, he wouldn't dream (he says) of condemning personal reverie' ...

After that one can't help wondering, not how sincere, but how *logical*, this notable scholar's attitude was to the method he recommends. He appears to be finding that clear distinctions and rational categories don't, after all, work equally well with every kind of literature, and that some of the major components of literature escape them altogether. What of the imagination? What of feeling and sensibility? The most astonishing thing in Lanson's defence is that he seems completely to ignore the claims of the aesthetic and the intuitive. Although he can pay lip-service to *le goût* and *le beau*, actually he had, by this time, turned his back on the claims of taste.

There is still one more of his reservations which I will myself reserve. It will go far toward suggesting a *new* method of the kind we want. Lanson saw the gleam but omitted to follow it up. We must attempt to do so ourselves.

A couple of thunderbolts have recently fallen on the conventional conception and practice of *l'explication française*, each proceeding from an interesting and *interested* source. The fact that they come from different grades of the hierarchy makes the simultaneity of their attacks all the more impressive. The first, I need scarcely say, is the *fons et origo* of our present interest in this topic. Professor Vinaver's stimulating criticism of the Method has already attracted much attention, nearly all of it, so far as I can judge, highly appreciative. To me, I confess, thinking of my long-fettered background, it has come like a breath of liberation.

No one before him has, so far as I know, brought out the fundamental flaw involved in its use. That is, the tendency to *over-rationalize* both the method itself and the very concept of literature to which it is applied. I feel particularly grateful to him for having directed the critical attention of his hearers, and (I hope) the critical humour of his subsequent readers, on to one of the most preposterous examples I know of pedantic and obtuse dogmatism—that phrase from Roustan's *Précis d'explication française*: 'Nous faisons pour décomposer le texte ce que l'auteur a fait pour le composer' . . . Can this mean other than one thing: that a schoolboy has only to reverse the order of Roustan's analysis to know how a piece of literature was composed? Shades of the prison-house! When one thinks of the amount of exquisite writing produced by the poets themselves in vain efforts to explain the mystery of their own creativity, what a waste of spirit in an expense of words it has all been! The secret is a trick of analysis in a pedant's manual. That one can, in a manner like Euclid's, lay down *a priori* an axiom or a set of axioms on what literature is and how it is made, and having with imperturbable assurance established this abstract basis, then deduce the qualities of a piece of real literature—this we must regard as the *reductio ad absurdum* of the method and of its supporters. Roustan's notion is a travesty, a caricature of the method extolled by Lanson and his disciples, but it should serve to remind us that they too were tainted with the false confidence of the rationalism of their age.

The second thunderclap is one that resounded in a French educational journal very soon after Professor Vinaver's address was delivered. The latter was inspired by aesthetic and philosophical apprehensions. The protest which was brought to my notice in the periodical called *l'Information littéraire* for January–February 1961, is signed by a *professeur de lycée* and receives strong support from an Inspecteur Général, who calls it 'un cri de souffrance et un acte d'accusation'. And it is both. But it is also a piece of well documented pedagogical criticism. The teacher-critic is outspoken, surprisingly so, I think, for a member of a closed educational system like the French. I have often noticed, by the way, how much more explicit French teachers can be on matters of educational interest than our own teachers are, or at least were when I was chief examiner some years ago. (The Higher literature paper, for instance, had been allowed to demand answers to ten questions in three hours, and I had the job of devil's advocate to reduce that total by one!)

The teacher-critic in the case before us begins with a root-and-branch attack on the curriculum, the examination and the methods of preparation at the *baccalauréat* level, and drives his points home with effective arguments and examples.[1] The *baccalauréat*, he says, is boosted as an examination in *culture générale*. In reality, as the results show, it is an excuse for cramming. The culprits, he maintains, are not the pupils but 'ourselves' who, despite all our impositions and exactions, make such a mediocre success of training the judgement. The first and main protest is against an overcrowded curriculum. This may not be of importance to us. But having pressed his attack home against the size of the syllabus and the amount of literary history it entails, the critic imagines himself being asked: 'But haven't you that well-tried tool (*cet outil éprouvé*), *l'explication française?*'

His answer is interesting. 'For cultivated adults it is, without doubt, an admirable exercise . . . But for adolescents who have yet to discover Pascal and Voltaire, how can one think that the *detailed explication*, as we practise it, can be the instrument of this discovery, and enable us to avoid the schematization that I am now denouncing? Let us see how the thing works. To study Voltaire, whose *œuvre* fills a huge library shelf, the manuals offer half a dozen pages: we teachers must summarize the rest. How can this be called *probité intellectuelle?*'

When it comes to the explication of the text (which is likely to be a rich anthology piece), the teacher has to elucidate its details by referring to *other* texts which the pupils are not likely to know. Try, for example, to make Montaigne known from a few extracts taken from the Third

---

[1] What follows is an epitome of the argument, freely translated or paraphrased.

Book of the Essays. The *professeur* supplies the connective tissue under pressure of time by a plunge into rhetoric which the bell puts an end to.

What do the pupils themselves say about this mode of procedure? And what does their weekly work show? '*Trop de richesses!*' they protest. 'Racine himself never premeditated the fine things you have ascribed to him.'

The microscope, the teacher goes on to say, is not the very first instrument that is used with beginners in science and the eyes of our pupils are not yet adapted to the beauties of the infinitesimal. To practise with them *l'explication française* 'in its official rigour and vigour' is only to put high pressure on the virtuosity of the teacher who enjoys his own performance, while the pupils, although they may applaud, feel that the spectacle doesn't concern them.[1]

And now comes what is for us the most pertinent point in the protest. What is the root cause, the teacher asks, of the trouble diagnosed? The harm, it is argued, comes essentially from a grave error at the beginning, the fact that our teaching of French has been conceived by literary scholars of the academic type (*universitaires lettrés*), on the model of what they are and of what they feel themselves. In the adolescents who are being initiated into literary studies, they have looked only for dwarf adults and academics in miniature, and they have imposed on them, through the teachers in the schools, a reduced model of (university) teaching and knowledge (*science*). What is needed is to *invent* for the pupils a specific method which would be made to suit them, but which would alone be capable of leading them to discover what we (their elders) admire ... We must renounce this kaleidoscope of bits and pieces that we pass before our pupils' eyes until it dazes them.

[1] Precisely the same defect as Lanson denounced in the teaching of taste referred to in chapter III.

The author of this *plainte* lays the blame ultimately on the fact that the method was contrived by learned academics, acting according to their own lights, and imposed upon the minds of the young to whom it is not suited. And we need not go far for evidence in support. In his defence Lanson himself gave the method a learned origin. 'Who invented this exercise?' he asks, and answers: 'The explication of texts is identical in essence with the *exegesis* practised in the religious sciences and in classical philology.' Its origins, then, are high and dry.

But let us not take this reproach too absolutely. It would be a bad thing for us all; it would divide off scholarship from teaching, if henceforth the teachers in the schools could not call upon those in the universities for assistance and guidance. Yet we all know that pressure from the universities can embarrass the schools, and that the danger is constant, and often commented on today, of sixth-formers being trained as if they were all going to be undergraduate prizemen, and of undergraduates being trained as if they were all going to be academic specialists!

Returning to our consideration of the formal exercise, we must glance at one more objection which is as serious as any. The method is an anachronism; it is out of date.

If I were asked what attitude of mind underlies the traditional form of it, I should reply that it is a form of logical analysis motivated by a rational inquiry. The questions it asks are conformable to the scientific rationalism that had swept over higher studies in France in the early years of this century, and which proceeded very largely from the Positivism of the last century. Going back to pick up Lanson's words—the demand for clear, precise and distinct ideas—is it not obvious that, in using them, he is directing attention to the rational elements in the piece of literature under treatment? And when we think of the categories which the method imposes, they too, obviously proceed from a rational scheme which is fixed, *a priori*, and to which the piece of literature, whether prose or poem, is expected to respond. But this is to presuppose an immobile, undeveloping literature, a *stable* poetry—which is a contradiction in terms.

Is there any kind of literature to which such a method is applicable? Yes; I think we could expect it to apply to literature of a marked rational type. Here we may feel safe for a moment. No national literature, it might be argued, is more rational (or more secular) on the whole than the literature of France has been through a large part of its course. But is this true of modern French literature? Professor Vinaver does not allow as much as I have done. 'No educated Frenchman of today', he says, 'with a feeling for great poetry and prose would apply to his own reading the method of analysis he once mastered at school. More than that, the process of literary appreciation usually has to wait until the last vestiges of the method have been effaced.' On the other hand, speaking of the *explicateurs* he says: 'They are hopelessly out of step with present-day aesthetic thought, dramatically out of step with all that is alive in contemporary criticism.'

And that is not simply a personal view. It happens that an objective answer to our question is available which will save us from any kind of special pleading. An elaborate, well documented answer is given by a French critic and man of letters of unusually wide and exact culture. I refer to the survey of recent tendencies by R.-M. Albérès: *L'Aventure intellectuelle du XXe siècle*, a revised edition of which appeared in 1959.[1] What M. Albérès reveals is the prevalence in our time of strong *anti*-intellectual currents, converging in a combined critical and sceptical assault on the older rational positions. His investigations tend to show that the

[1] See Appendix, p. 190.

major literatures of this half century, including French literature since about 1880 are riven with irruptions of the Irrational. And surely nothing could be truer of the poetry written in France during this period, the whole urge of which tends to get away from anything like imitation, or even recognition, of the rationally controlled productions of the seventeenth and eighteenth centuries, and to revert to the intuitive sources of primitive impulse, to the rich chaos of unconscious motivation, and above all to fantasy, free association and fresh, spontaneous sensation. Nothing characterizes these movements better than the headlines or nicknames associated with them: Symbolism, Surrealism, Anti-intellectualism, *L'Homme révolté, l'Absurde*. . . .

Of these, Symbolism would best serve our purpose to conclude this discussion, as it is essentially a poetical movement and is likely to be better known than the subsequent manifestations of the modern muse.

The Symbolist type of poem is anything but a structure of clear and distinct ideas. Here indeed the well-known remark made by Mallarmé to Degas comes in most aptly: 'You don't make poetry out of ideas but out of words.' Logic, explicit statement, descriptive narrative, allegory, eloquence are all traditional poetical assets which the Symbolists (Mallarmé himself and a couple of generations of his admirers) rejected and disallowed. What then is left? Lanson supplied the answer, as it were, *en passant*.

Earlier I mentioned a further reservation of his, which I would keep for the end. I will translate it literally: 'This is not to say that, in the presence of a work of literature, *and all the more so if it is removed in type from science and approaches music*, each one of us cannot have his individual reaction, and it is perfectly legitimate for it to be quite a personal one. . . .'[1] The omnivorous reader that Lanson was must have

[1] My italics.

known that, in this distinction between science and music, there was a world of new possibilities for the appreciation of modern poetry, and perhaps of all true lyricism. But the hint is dropped as if it had no significance.

Even one hundred years ago a most interesting and pertinent example had appeared among some new poems added to the second edition of *Les Fleurs du Mal*. Turn to *Le Cygne* (in *Les Tableaux Parisiens*) and compare the structure of the poem with the way a symphony or a sonata, or a Wagnerian overture, is composed on a basis of recurrent themes and interwoven motifs—recurring, notice, not according to a regular pattern as in a hymn tune, but obeying the intuitive impulse that dictates the more varied musical forms. Following this hint, you may be just as precise as you wish in explaining such a poem and find you can account for all its significant elements, without invoking any of the stereotyped categories which were not designed for creations of this kind.[1]

And now I should like to risk drawing a few examples from the poems and thought of Mallarmé. The risk is that you might think—as some teachers I addressed a few years ago appeared to think—that the upshot of my talk was to persuade you to teach more Mallarmé to your pupils. But not at all! I am only going to indicate some of the novelties he and a few of his contemporaries introduced, many of which have become characteristic or recurrent—for good or ill—in modern poetry.

In approaching poetry of this type the young reader may be helped to face the difficulties it presents by first being reminded that the innovating poet tries to discover new potentialities in language, to extend the limits of grammar and

[1] See chapter VIII. Another example from Baudelaire of an even earlier date is the celebrated poem, *La Chevelure*. Such poems should be treated for what they are and not used to exhibit a pedagogical method.

perhaps also to relax the rules of prosody. As Vaugelas in the seventeenth century assumed, the grammarian is not the maker of language but the observer and recorder of its usage. It is the people who speak it and write it who create or recreate a language. In cases like Mallarmé, Rimbaud, Laforgue and lesser innovators certain traits, which the purist might still, with good reason, condemn as *defects* of expression, have been turned to the service of a new conception of poetic art. The reader who comes to their work for the first time should be prepared for at least three things that may be worth tabulating.

First, complex and involved types of imagery based on the comparison or *rapprochement* of terms which show no clear resemblance. Secondly, a serene disregard of the rule that forbids the mixing of metaphors. And thirdly, a degree of concentration or *contraction* in the images that are sometimes crowded and crushed together in a way that deranges the normal order of words and disrupts the syntax. And we must add one more disconcerting feature. Mallarmé was a forerunner in the acceptance of Ambiguity as a deliberate literary device. That is, he recognized that words and phrases may be capable of more than one interpretation, and he sometimes plays on a number of meanings derived from the same group of vocables. This can be disturbing to the pupil who has hitherto been trained to an exact use of language and bred in the practice of rational or logical modes of thought. Such correct modes, he will, of course, always need to cultivate. But he will now have to face the fact that much poetry from Mallarmé's time depends on a more intuitive use of language than has been customary in the past, a use that obeys (as it is often said) the 'logic of music' rather than the logic of rational thought and speech.

To sum up, the late nineteenth century was a period of great experimentation in all the arts including literature.

Not only did unprecedented novelties occur in the use of language, but disruptions of the traditional forms and kinds of poetry opened the way to new possibilities of rhythmical expression which are still being exploited. The *typographical* distinctions that it had hitherto been customary to expect between poetry and prose were often ignored, and following Baudelaire's example, poets like Mallarmé and Rimbaud wrote an increasing number of their poems in prose. Gradually it came to be recognized that the rhythms of poetry cannot be perpetually confined within the range of the traditional metres, and that effective liberties could be taken with the accepted stanza patterns. The most fundamental change attempted in French rhythm was to escape from a mode of prosody or versification, in which scansion was based on the count of syllables, and to experiment in rhythms dictated solely by the pulse of the poet's feeling or the breath of his inspiration.

'On a touché au vers,' Mallarmé exclaimed when the first *vers libres* appeared. But although he gave the new form his blessing, Mallarmé insisted that the 'official verse', as he called the alexandrine, should always be available for full-organ effects. And we teachers must not forget to tell the younger generation that few innovations have ever put an abrupt end to long-respected traditions. So it has been in France. If Claudel uses a *verset* for his odes that reminds one both of the versicle of the Psalms and of Whitman's 'lawless line', Valéry revives the strict decasyllabic for *Le Cimetière Marin*. And in each case the genius of the poet confirms the choice of the form, whether novel or traditional.

We must be prepared to extend our interests and to exercise our adaptive responses, looking closely at the new ventures of the last seventy or eighty years, observing them carefully for what they are, and trying to perceive what the authors were striving to bring off. This will stretch the resilience of our sensibilities and exercise the springs of perception in our pupils and students—and ourselves. Live poetry and the arts never stand and wait upon modes of explication. The curiosity of a later generation is not likely to remain within the limits of our own intelligence and taste, however far we stretch them. It won't do, you know, to let our pupils and students completely outdistance us in the approach to the arts of the time we live together in! Nor will it do to allow a narrow scientific rationalism to contradict the poet who said: 'Beauty is truth, truth beauty.'

VII

THE ENGLISH APPROACH TO RONSARD[1]

After a life of unexampled celebrity for a poet, Pierre de Ronsard was almost forgotten in France for over two centuries, no edition of his works having appeared between 1629 and 1857. During the seventeenth and eighteenth centuries, despite the protests of a dwindling line of defenders, his poetry was grudgingly represented in an occasional anthology or casually disparaged by an occasional critic, echoing the aspersions of Malherbe and Boileau. The characteristic attitude, though not at first universal, became one of neglect, indifference, even disdain for a barbarous ancestor, whose 'pitoyables poésies', in the great Arnauld's phrase, it was incumbent upon national self-esteem to disown and ignore. When at rare moments the shrug of the shoulders yielded to articulate fault-finding, we hear of Ronsard's injuries to style, his turgid rhetoric, his provincial jargon, his unreadableness. Ronsard had plumed himself too seriously on being the *poète né*. His censors mocked at his *fureur*, just as more recently harsh critics have scoffed at the inspired frenzy or the ubiquitous 'genius' of the Romantics. True, he knew something of the ancients. Perhaps too much. His commerce with them lacked reticence, not to say reverence. He was too wildly enthusiastic, too indiscriminating,

---

[1] First published in the *Criterion* for July 1933. Since it was intended as a contribution to the 'classic or romantic' discussion of that time, I have left it in its original form.

too indiscreet—a Vandal, returning with arms full of ill-assorted spoils and embarrassed with the task of setting them off decently in his 'gothic' palace of art.

Nous avons changé tout cela. It is his critics of the classical period, whom nowadays we scorn for their obtuseness, their narrowness of taste. Incomprehensible in their failure to acknowledge the forerunner, they appear almost despicable in their ignorant exaggeration of what they deemed to be the clumsy, unassimilated classicism of their victim. M. Jusserand has pointed out that the uncontrolled side of Ronsard's cult of the ancients is nearly always illustrated from his one failure, the abandoned experiment in epic. It was to the ill-starred *Franciade* that he affixed those unfortunate and almost popular lines:

> Les François qui ces vers liront,
> S'ils ne sont et Grecs et Romains,
> En lieu de mon livre ils n'auront
> Qu'un pesant faix entre les mains.

As in most matters of taste and aesthetics, the Romantics have run counter to the Classics here. They have done more than rehabilitate a forgotten poet; they have resuscitated a buried one. A great achievement, certainly. But as we follow the stages of their effort, a grave doubt seizes and grows upon us. Romantic critics, poets and scholars have combined to recall a sixteenth-century poet from the dead. But is that poet Pierre de Ronsard? 'They took Ronsard for their Bible,' said George Wyndham. It is to be feared, rather, that, having so to speak established a loose, but by no means disinterested, liaison with their 'divin ressuscité', most of them left him there, a Bible unread.

Superb egoists, those Romanticists of 1830 were the last of men to undertake the spadework necessary in a humanly managed resurrection, without good personal reasons and a possibility of returns. In unearthing and extolling Ronsard they were looking for a tradition, a *romantic* tradition in pre-classic times. But was Ronsard in the least a Romantic? For nearly a century poets and critics have been appraising him from the aesthetic angle characteristic of their milieu— applauding him for his difference from the Classics, condemning him for his difference from the Romantics. Admitted by all to be frequently a charming artist, Ronsard has been pitied for having missed greatness through lack of 'passion' and 'power'. His *fureur* pales to a thin flame beside the blaze of Romantic fire. There is an absence of intimacy in his work—not a whit of soul-searching inwardness, no plunging depth of pessimism, no heaven-scaling audacity of Promethean challenge. How, indeed, could he be a fervent and fiery poet, when he is so learned and derivative a one? Let us beware of asking too much of this simple-minded 'amateur' . . .

Much Pléiade criticism has been vitiated by such prejudices as these. Defects due to judging Ronsard by contemporary standards are conspicuous even in the praises of his admirers. They are prominent in Pater.

The famous essay on Joachim Du Bellay was recommended by Mr Richard Aldington as the best possible introduction to Du Bellay. But in so far as it treats of Ronsard, it offers more than one instance of the danger of a kind of bias, characteristic of late nineteenth-century criticism. Pater starts by insisting, with an emphasis which prejudices his case, upon the *medievalism* of Renaissance art and literature. The poetry of the French Renaissance is a gothic survival masquerading in plumes borrowed from Italy. The object of Ronsard's revolution was to accept 'that influx of Renaissance taste which, leaving the . . . poetry of France at bottom what it was, old French Gothic still, gilds its surface with a strange, delightful, foreign aspect passing over all that northern land, in itself neither deeper nor more permanent than a chance effect of light'.

Pater evidently clung to the conception of the old as fundamental and the new as façade. For him the poetry of the French Renaissance would not be comparable with Chambord, which was a new building with certain ornamental reminiscences; it would be more like Ronsard's home, La Possonnière, a small castle in the old style, superficially altered by the poet's father to conform to the numerous fashionable palaces springing up in the neighbourhood. Early Romanticism having everywhere been associated with, and stimulated by, a revival of medieval interests, one wonders how far this orientation may not be implied generally in the nineteenth-century attitude to the question of origins, and to what extent it may underlie the tendency we find in one of the greatest of Romantic critics to overestimate the medieval, at the expense of the classical, strain in the work of Ronsard.

George Wyndham questioned Pater's sweeping statement over a quarter of a century ago. The essay on *Ronsard and La Pléiade* might have been written as a protest. But at that time the matter could not be handled either fully or surely, and Wyndham admitted that he was inviting inquiry rather than seeking to deliver a judgement. On one important point he may have been mistaken. Wyndham held Sainte-Beuve responsible for the view which Pater was to profess.[1] But it is difficult to see how Pater could have been relying on the *Tableau de la Poésie française au XVIe siècle*, without assuming that he had read it somewhat cursorily. The French critic's final judgement on Ronsard's effort concludes with these terms of reproach: 'Au lieu de rentrer franchement au sein des traditions nationales et de réinstaller notre littérature dans sa portion légitime du patri-

[1] George Wyndham, *Essays in Romantic Literature*, p. 82.

moine légué par le moyen âge, il avait imaginé follement d'envahir l'antiquité.'[1] This implies just the opposite view from Pater's. But Sainte-Beuve also claimed that Ronsard, in the less ambitious and better part of his work, had recovered the poetic language of Marot. He was careful, however, to explain that Ronsard achieved this through changing his antique model from Pindar to poets of the Anacreon type, who happened to be nearer in spirit to the French tradition.[2]

This has been the line followed with great thoroughness by subsequent scholarship and criticism. The main thesis of M. Laumonier's important work, *Ronsard, poète lyrique*, is to establish the fact implied in the question raised in the *avant-propos*: '*N'a-t-il pas, quoi qu'il en ait dit, des obligations certaines à la poésie médiévale et marotique?*' After full inquiry, the answer is overwhelmingly in the affirmative. Ronsard's very earliest odes, written to emulate Marot's *Psaumes* in form though not in spirit, are compared, by the critic, to the best of Lemaire, Marot and Saint-Gelais. They were followed by the '*erreur historique*' of Pindaric imitation and the break with the school of Marot; after which Ronsard reverted to the '*inspiration marotique*' by cultivating a series of more congenial models; the Greek Anthology, Anacreon, Catullus, Marullus and other neo-Latin poets.

This line of argument had already been suggested by Sainte-Beuve. But it could hardly be this, or anything like this, that Pater meant by 'a blending of Italian ornament with the general outline of Northern influence'. M. Laumonier nowhere denies the importance of antique as well as contemporary influences, the thorough cultivation of which by Ronsard brought him back, almost involuntarily, to the native tradition. Nor must it be forgotten, as another

[1] Sainte-Beuve, *Tableau de la Poésie française au seizième siècle* (Nouvelle édition), p. 165.
[2] Ibid., p. 75, note 2.

recent critic has maintained, that Ronsard did not merely continue, even when he was most deeply indebted. He constantly instilled new life into old forms: '*Il commençait un art nouveau.*'[1]

A more serious fault of Pater's is to have misjudged the spirit of the sixteenth-century poet and his work, as a consequence of having looked at them through tinged lenses of of his own prescription. Was not Pater, however much he deprecated the suggestion, the chief formulator of the *fin de siècle* aesthetic, with its predilection for the decorative and its cult of a type of beauty, languorous, valetudinarian, insidiously decadent? It is interesting to watch how such an ideal emasculates and denaturalizes a kind of poetry which has more exuberant youth and adventurous impulse in it than has anything written during the later 'Renaissance of Wonder', with more healthy vigour and sanguine assurance than will be found in all the lyrical outpourings of the 'Century of Hope'.

Ronsard became deaf at sixteen: and it was this circumstance which finally determined him to be a man of letters instead of a diplomatist, significantly, one might fancy, of a certain premature agedness, and of the tranquil, temperate sweetness appropriate to that, in the school of poetry which he founded. Its charm is that of a thing not vigorous or original, but full of the grace which comes of long study and reiterated refinements, and many steps repeated, and many angles worn down, with an exquisite faintness, *une fadeur exquise*—a certain tenuity and caducity, as for those who can hear nothing vehement or strong; for princes weary of love, like Francis the First, or of pleasure, like Henry the Third, or of action, like Henry the Fourth. Its merits are those of the old—grace and finish, perfect in minute detail. For these people are a little jaded, and have a constant desire for a subdued and delicate excitement, to warm their creeping fancy a little.

[1] H. Franchet, *Le poète et son œuvre d'après Ronsard*, p. 265.

Far from being the exquisite, otiose, prematurely senile existence imagined by the suave English critic, the life of Pierre de Ronsard seems, according to the more virile portraiture of recent scholarship, to have been the wholesome, easy, but by no means inactive life of a French country gentleman of the Renaissance, intermittently a courtier, always a Prince of poets, preferring, on the whole, to the luxurious *entourage* of the monarch, a kind of semi-retirement shared between the countrysides around Vendôme and the riversides of Touraine and Anjou, yet with a finger on the feverish pulse of his time, freely partaking of all that nature, beauty, a smiling though not lavish fortune had to offer, and at the beginning and end of each full, calm day, thanking God for the munificence of His gifts, not forgetting to recommend to His care the land in its sore distress, the cause of his lord, the king, and of his lady, the Church. Grace but not languor, a graceful and unstinted enjoyment of existence, rather than an impassioned weariness of living, and above all, manliness, are his marks. One of the sanest conceptions of life realized by a man of the Renaissance was his. For Ronsard's ideal was not set beyond his grasp. Life for him was not an impossible romance nor an unattainable saintliness. Yet an ideal which does not include martyrdom need not exclude service. And Ronsard's rule for life, as for art, was the Horatian *moins et meilleur*—something less lofty than the inaccessible, and perhaps better, because capable of becoming concrete and real. His fundamental conception of poetry as an ardent and even youthful enthusiasm, indirectly adopted from Plato, refutes the notion of *fadeur exquise*. Poetry was the flower of 'virtue', which in the idealism of the time meant the total excellence of the nobleman. The poet was an aristocrat; he was not an aesthete. George Wyndham was certainly right when he forbade us to think 'that Ronsard, or any of his companions, evaded the conditions of their age to indulge in the languid fallacy of art for art's sake'.

Recent critical distinctions and the skirmishes that have passed between the protagonists of the two great traditions seem to have brought out one characteristic of interest to our theme—the strong associative element present in all Romantic art and literature, and the importance of emotional association for the Romantic critic. For over a century it has been a fallacy of popular taste and a presumption of serious criticism to take the specific types of romantic emotion as the *sine qua non* of all poetry. This perhaps may explain how it is that Mr Arthur Tilley, one of our academic authorities on the literature of the French Renaissance, could have read the charming *Amours* of Ronsard with so little appreciation of the radical difference between two distinct types of amorous poetry as to have given the following verdict:

Apart from superiority in language and rhythm, there is nothing to distinguish this volume (*Amours de Cassandre*) from the other *Amours*, or series of love sonnets in imitation of Petrarch, which were produced at this time with such wearisome reiteration. They have all the same three faults: coldness, insincerity, monotony. It has been said that the coldness is due to the fact that they are addressed to ideal mistresses. But an imaginary passion, if it is also imaginative, can and does produce passionate poetry. Rather the coldness is to be ascribed to the same cause as the insincerity, to the fact that Ronsard and his fellows modelled themselves on a poet with whose feelings as a lover they had no sympathy. Ordinary sensual men, they used the language of spiritual love; lovers of a day, they imitated a man who loved for eternity. Their monotony is equally easy of explanation. Their theme was one which only the intensity of passion can save from being monotonous. When passion is absent and the poet has nothing but poetic machinery to fall back on, then the allegory, the mythological learning, the antithesis, the points and puns of Petrarch become wearisome.[1]

What more unfortunate introduction for an Englishman approaching Ronsard? It flatters his native taste for moral distinctions in aesthetic matters by over-emphasizing an antithesis, not unreal perhaps, but certainly misleading, between the 'sensual' Pléiade and their spiritual model. Ignoring the difference in tone between the *Cassandre* volume and those that follow, wherein a genial, frankly *gaulois*, epicureanism becomes increasingly prominent, it confuses these sonnets with the output of the rest of Ronsard's group, in which the licentious element sometimes predominates at the expense of everything else. Certainly if one read all the *Amours* in succession, one would get, and deserve to get, the surfeit of reiteration promised by the English scholar. It would be a dull taste, however, that failed to distinguish Ronsard's from the rest. Even Mr Middleton Murry, whose essay on Ronsard in *Aspects of Literature* could not be called enthusiastic, would agree on this point. 'However much,' he writes, 'one may tire of him, the fatigue is never infected by the nausea which is produced by some of the mechanical sonnet sequences of his contemporaries.'

The *Amours de Cassandre* are, it is true, indebted for much of their material to Petrarch and Bembo; they are loaded with mythological allusion to the point of being frequently obscure. For the edition of 1578 the author sanctioned a running commentary by his friend Muret, which still renders a service to the text. But within the limits set by these models, the sonnets are remarkable for their variety of tone and device, for the immediate charm of most of them and for the brilliant success of many. M. Laumonier considers that this collection contains 'a pretty good number of

[1] Arthur Tilley, *The Literature of the French Renaissance*, vol. 1, p. 328.

very fine sonnets, some of which are hardly inferior to those of Petrarch'.[1] The contrast in tone which has been suggested between the French sonnets and their Italian prototypes is more invidious than valid. It would be a critical error to present these poems as the work of a sensual man. Ronsard himself conceived of his imitations of Petrarch as tending, among other things, to *elevate* French amorous poetry.[2] Nowhere perhaps do they reach the pure Petrarchan heights, but as M. Pierre de Nolhac says, they are inspired by a chaste, youthful idealism, which is precisely what distinguishes them from the rest of their author's amorous verse. And although they may show no passion in the Romantic sense, they are not devoid of a certain kind of passion, even when it is conveyed, as here, through a blend of Petrarchan reminiscence and Platonic myth:

> Qu'Amour mon cœur, qu'Amour mon ame sonde,
> Luy qui cognoist ma seule intention,
> Il trouvera que toute passion
> Veufve d'espoir, par mes veines abonde.
>   Mon Dieu, que j'aime, est-il possible au monde
> De voir un cœur si plein d'affection,
> Pour la beauté d'une perfection,
> Qui m'est dans l'ame en playe si profonde?
>   Le cheval noir qui ma Royne conduit,
> Suyvant le traq où ma chair la seduit,
> A tant erré d'une vaine traverse,
>   Que j'ay grand peur (si le blanc ne contraint
> Sa course folle, et ses pas ne refraint
> Dessous le joug) que ma raison ne verse. (XXI)

---

[1] *Ronsard, poète lyrique*, p. 482, note 4.
[2] M. Laumonier shows how Ronsard nursed the hope and ambition to surpass his French forerunners, who are described in the poet's manner as 'trop enflés, ou énervés, ou amoureux d'une dame paillarde' . . . op. cit., p. 479. Another French authority prefers to speak of Ronsard's *emulation* of Petrarch. See H. Longnon, *Pierre de Ronsard*, 1912, p. 349, note 2.

Far from being cold pieces of monotonous mechanism, sonnets like this one are in their own way the personal productions of an artist, first and foremost, but of an artist who was no less a lover—'amours d'artiste', says M. Franchet, 'mais amours imprudents dont il a très visiblement souffert' . . .[1]

This brings us to the root of all these differences—the radical opposition of aesthetic standard and critical standpoint which can make such poems as these of Ronsard unpalatable and wearisome to Romantic taste, and can render Romantic criticism indifferent or blind to the special merits of poems which it seems all the more anxious to appreciate, because they are the work of a poet in the glory of whose rediscovery it claims a monopoly.

The judgement quoted above is not mistaken so much as inappropriate. Ronsard's *Amours* are a triumph of literary art. This, their real value, is passed over as mere superiority in language and rhythm. Yet it is beauty not passion which is, after all, the true source of their inspiration and of their peculiar originality. For, according to the theory of the Pléiade, as M. de Nolhac has pointed out,[2] originality consisted in giving a subject a French form and not in the subject itself or in its development. This was borrowed from antiquity or from Italy, as from a common fund, whence everybody had already drawn and would again draw without scruple. It is the style, the movement, the new adaptation that count, and all notion of plagiarism goes by the board. Ronsard and his disciples glory in having borrowed something fine from another language. For them this is a conquest, and Muret's commentary on his friend's sonnets notes with complacency in every passage the application of this doctrine as so much to Ronsard's

[1] Op. cit., p. 231.
[2] Preface to Garnier's edition of the Complete Works of Ronsard.

credit, so much also to the debt which the French nation owes to him. Muret rendered a great service in treating Ronsard as a difficult author, but the work in question had enough life in it to obtain a durable success and, as M. de Nolhac insists, the life in it was precisely the amount of himself that Ronsard had put into the expression of his love.

M. de Nolhac develops this point in a paragraph which might almost have been written to refute the English verdict. I have italicized a word or two which are in marked contrast to the accusations of unoriginality, coldness and insincerity:

> Parmi les poètes de l'amour, Ronsard tient rang d'*inventeur*. Il use de modèles littéraires, de parures mythologiques, des thèmes platoniciens de Pétrarque et de Bembo; mais *c'est la vérité d'une passion jeune, ardente, sincère, qui se livre en ses premiers recueils*, comme se révélera dans les Sonnets pour Hélène la mélancolie des dernières tendresses. A travers les lieux communs de la rhétorique amoureuse et sous la convention des symboles, s'évoque *la beauté des femmes qui ont régné sur un cœur fervent; ils retracent des aventures réelles, les drames véridiques de l'espoir, de l'indifférence, de l'infidélité ou de la séparation.*

At a risk of presenting the Cassandre volume simply as a triumph of virtuosity, we must emphasize the sheer sudden mastery over the arts of poetic expression which, along with the first *Odes*, it so abundantly illustrates. What an amazing, almost facile command of the riches of antique imagery! What exultation, what *romance* there must have been for its author in the versatile exercise of the newly acquired art! To pass from Marot to Ronsard is to pass in one generation from the late Middle Ages to the full Renaissance; and if Marot be claimed as a poet of the Renaissance, then Ronsard, as an artist, is our contemporary. 'Son vers a déjà toutes nos musiques, et c'est lui qui a orchestré nos rythmes pour un concert qui n'est pas près de finir.'[1]

There is a point to be considered in judging the poetry of another age which seems rarely to have occurred to the critics of a century justly proud of its historical sense. To use terminology of a recent vogue, all poetry is symbolical. It expresses, conveys or suggests something incommunicable save by emblems and 'indirections'. Each age has its favourite mode or formula which serves better than another to present the contemporary mind with the reality symbolized. The mode or formula which seemed vital to one age may lack power of suggestion for another. Most revolutionary poets appear conventional to their successors. Before his death, the descendants of that arch-rebel, Victor Hugo, were smashing through his conventions and lamenting his timidity. Today scholars can talk complacently of Hugo's classicism.

Are we not therefore justified in asking whether the particular convention of Ronsard's poetry may not have seemed as vital to his contemporaries as the Romantic convention seemed to the nineteenth-century mind? Ronsard was certainly as living a poet for his readers as Hugo was for his. He was royally flattered and universally acclaimed with an enthusiasm which might have satisfied even the exorbitant author of *Les Châtiments*. If he was also a more *learned* poet, that is surely a compliment to those who could appreciate him. And they must have been numerous. For one may well hesitate to agree with J. C. Bailey, who in *The Claims of French Poetry* spoke of the Renaissance as an 'age which could not be expected to distinguish between fine words and great poetry'. Is it not possible that the sixteenth-century poet could run into the mould of the Petrarchan sonnet an

[1] Pierre de Nolhac, op. cit.

emotion really felt, and that his reader could experience, if not a Romantic *frisson*, at least a *romanesque* thrill in recognizing it there? The immense popularity of Ronsard and his school leads us to suppose that this was probable.[1]

It is clear that the poets and their readers grew tired of the glut of *pétrarquisme*. Du Bellay wrote *Contre les Pétrarquistes* and, with Ronsard, resorted to the practice of a more direct art. But the wave of Petrarch's influence returned with Desportes and its tide remained high for the rest of the century. And for all its derivativeness, it is not justly characterized as 'an imitation of a poet with whose feeling as a lover they had no sympathy'. Petrarch, it is true, was platonic and the group of the Pléiade were no doubt nearer the level of the *homme moyen sensuel*. But if this is a mark of their inferiority as men, it may be their distinction as artists, and the secret of their originality. It was certainly this touch of nature that made them akin to their contemporaries.

But in speculating upon the sort of 'thrill' produced by the content and associations of his poetry, we ourselves are regarding Ronsard with Romantic eyes. May not his poetry, his early poetry at least, belong to a distinct and separate category—what a post-Romantic critic might be excused for calling a 'pure' type of poetry, not dependent for its effect on the associative power of its content, yet not inferior in beauty for those who had—and have—the taste for it? And may not the whole body of Renaissance lyricism, from the sonnets of Petrarch to the sonnets of Shakespeare, conform to this type? It is the nineteenth century that has

[1] M. Laumonier discussed the point—how far sincerity of the emotions is compatible with their expression by means of literary reminiscence—in his *Ronsard, poète lyrique* (pp. 475-6, and especially footnote, p. 476). We find that he forestalled our conclusion twenty years ago, quoting in support a phrase from E. Faguet: 'Un humaniste pleure sincèrement un être cher avec une réminiscence classique, comme un dévot le pleure profondément avec une citation des livres saints.'

shown most concern about W. H. and the Dark Lady. Just as it is the critics of that century—some of them at least—who were most sensitive to the absence of a passion for Cassandre from the odes and sonnets inspired by her name. The contemporaries of Ronsard and of Shakespeare were probably more susceptible than were readers of a later generation, to the purer forms of beauty. They found in the poetry of Ronsard, along with an echo of their own thoughts and feelings, a lyrical counterpart of that perfection of grace, charm and fancy which they perceived in the decorations of Fontainebleau or in the workmanship of a Cellini vase. Not that the Pléiade's ideal was a plastic beauty. The school of Ronsard was far nearer to that of Verlaine, with its cult of music, than to that of Gautier and Leconte de Lisle, with its love of enamels and statuary. Yet Ronsard was as little a Symbolist as he was a Parnassian. It would be best to call him simply a poet of the Renaissance, which is a category, almost a genre in itself. But if we must place him with either the Ancients or the Moderns, he is assuredly a classical poet, the first in France, and as a lyrist, perhaps the finest. He is no more Romantic than André Chénier. And if the seventeenth-century poets disowned him it is because, in one sense, he was nearer the source of Classicism than they were. He had more of the genial humanity of the Ancients, less of his successors' exclusive decorum and dry severity. Reason was not his god. Passion was not his master. As Pierre Champion affirms, he had Intelligence, which is, after all, the supreme classic virtue.[1]

A last authoritative word awaits us from the poet himself. Nothing brings out more clearly the essential classicality of Ronsard, that which differentiates him for all time from the Romanticists, than his chosen motto, taken from Horace, proclaimed as a corrective to the 'Romantic' tendencies of

[1] *Ronsard et son temps:* Introduction.

his time and treasured as a light guiding him to perfection—
Moins et meilleur. This phrase is the master key to the appreciation of his work. It should be forgotten least of all by those who approach its temperate reflections of the Vendômois, after a pilgrimage through the foggy sublimities and grandiose disproportions of the romantic North.

VIII

BAUDELAIRE'S POEM, 'LE CYGNE'
AN ESSAY IN COMMENTARY

LE CYGNE is one of the three central pieces that characterize and differentiate the *Tableaux Parisiens*. You will no doubt remember that these are a group of thirteen poems which were inserted, as a new section, into the second edition of *Les Fleurs du Mal*. This edition (which is the one usually favoured in preference to the first edition) Baudelaire himself saw through the press in 1861. Not all the pieces that compose it were written after the condemnation of the edition of 1857; but most of them, including all the best, were produced to make up for those poems that had been suppressed as a result of the trial. The 'pièces condamnées' amounted to half a dozen and, as the new poems are above that number, the trial could not justly be described as an ill wind that blew no one any good.

Le Cygne and the two poems that follow, *Les Sept Vieillards* and *Les Petites Vieilles*, form a trilogy of Baudelaire's most impressive productions. Mr T. S. Eliot appears to have a preference for them: they show supremely well what he distinguished as Baudelaire's special gift, a *sense of his own age*.[1] The phrase was first used by Mr Peter Quennell. One of the things it implies here is an awareness of the condition, physical and spiritual, of suffering humanity as found in the modern city; or better perhaps the tragedy of human beings exposed to misfortune as the poet perceived

[1] See his study of *Baudelaire* collected in *Selected Essays*.

them around him. Notice, first, in these poems the realism of observation and, particularly in *Le Cygne*, the exact location: the precincts of the Louvre. The milieu in all these tableaux is the Parisian scene—Paris, not as the capital of France, but as the great city, not quite the 'City of Dreadful Night', but the stage of the real yet common tragedies of life.

And don't miss the way the realistic vision is raised to high tension by a sense of mystery—mystery in the human condition—what is unfathomable in the fate of men and women, especially when their fate is most enigmatic, as in the case of the innocent doomed to destitution. A magnificent example of the poetic treatment of this case is the third of the trilogy, *Les Petites Vieilles*. Of parts of this poem Proust suggested that art could go no further in that direction.

It is, then, the fusion of realism and vision that distinguishes these poems. They reveal the gift *par excellence* of sublimation as characterized by Baudelaire himself in an alexandrine which he offered to the Deity in justification of his life and art:

> Tu m'as donné ta boue et j'en ai fait de l'or.

Let us look more closely into the realism. Most of these poems are studies of passers-by, loafers and streetwalkers. The words *passant*, *passer* recur. Some of them are figures that could better be called common rather than commonplace (none are commonplace in the poet's vision); some are spectral figures, formidable, fantastic yet haunting (*Les Sept Vieillards*); and one or two are beautiful. The theme of the 'œillade' is transformed into a remarkably fine sonnet, *A une Passante*. But none of these gripping or alluring apparitions is a sleep-walker or a dreamer, a mere ghost or fiction of the poet's brain: they are all real people circulating, alive and conscious, in the streets of the city.

And let us note another differentia. Despite the glamorous apparition of *la Passante* and that still more surprising figure, the female skeleton in the piece called *Danse macabre*, this section, the *Tableaux Parisiens*, is not concerned with the poet's love affairs. The feminine interest as such plays a very minor role and the torment of sex no role at all. Nor do Baudelaire's disconsolate moods return for treatment. Nothing here corresponds to those poetic studies of Ennui, the deadliest sin, which you find towards the end of the preceding section, *Spleen et Idéal*—a section that should logically have been called, *Idéal et Spleen*, to suggest the degeneration from the ideal, which the sequence of poems actually symbolizes.

To sum up, the *Tableaux Parisiens* are not concerned *directly* with their author himself. They are, most of them, new works offering vistas of still wider potentialities, which were never realized. The best of the series make one regret that Baudelaire's death precluded more poems of their kind. They show him emerging from the maelstrom of agonized introspection, liberated too from the exhaustion and despondency that followed excesses, the dissipation of energies and gifts, and the disappointments of the trial. He is now, if never before, the poet with a sense of his age. Not that the new view of life is at all optimistic: it is the *outlook* that has changed. Henceforth Baudelaire looks away from his own problems to envisage those shared by other human beings in a world of good and evil, of more evil than good, and therefore all the more alluring.

Now for *Le Cygne*. This poem is interesting for two things: (1) its variations of tone; (2) its singularity of form. Together these features make it exceptional among Baudelaire's poems and stamp it, I think, as an experiment of great significance in the development of form in modern French poetry. I am even going to suggest that similar developments in the poetic technique of other nations which were influenced by the French may find one of their sources here.

The tone of a poem is a difficult feature to define or analyse, however distinctly we may feel it. Here then we might take a hint from the scholars and inquire about the pertinent facts of the case. Are there any facts that throw light on the composition of this piece of verse?

Note that *Le Cygne* and the other two pieces of this trilogy are dedicated to Victor Hugo. When they were sent to the elder poet, who was then in exile, Baudelaire told him how much impressed he had been by certain compassionate poems Hugo had written, in which deep feeling was combined with colloquial language. Now is not that combination precisely what we have here? We seem to have found the *mot de l'énigme* on the poet's lips. And we may recall that in a recent letter to Baudelaire Hugo had expressed a compliment that has become famous: 'You have endowed the heaven of art with a ray of the macabre.' This reference does not, it is true, apply to *Le Cygne*: but it fits perfectly *Les Sept Vieillards*, and the operative word recurs in the poem called *Danse macabre*.

Deep objective compassion is one of the most moving and inspiring notes in art; but only the greatest artists and poets excel at expressing it. Shakespeare, Rembrandt and Beethoven, in particular, are revered for this kind of resonance detected in their works. And I suggest that in these three studies Baudelaire is second to none as a poet of compassionate feeling working *within the limits of lyrical form*— which are the characteristic limits of the best imaginative literature of the nineteenth century, a century that never rose to the height of great drama.

What makes this note so impressive? The strength and quality of feeling behind it, no doubt. But that is tautology.

The true explanation of its force, I think, lies in the *objectivity* with which the feeling is expressed. Compassion seems to be most effectively presented in great works of art by avoiding the *direct* expression of sympathy. In other words sympathy is an emotion which normally passes direct, like an electric current, from one individual to another. The good Samaritan, for instance, showed active sympathy for the injured man fallen on the wayside by crossing the road to help him; and the parable is an explicit method of conveying the moral straight to the heart. But great poetry does not work in this obvious way. Artistic compassion is usually less immediate in its application and more general in the range of its significance. The problem for the artist is to keep the generality of the vision infused with deep feeling and yet to restrain the feeling from flowing over into vague expansive sentiment, into mere effusion or *épanchement*, as the French call it. And the restraint which controls and directs strong feeling is a sign of great artistic effort.

But how is this to be effected in the poem? How is deep and powerful yet broad, objective feeling to be preserved from modes of expression that are too patently expressive? And how, at the same time, is the broad, strong feeling to be kept from the dilution of too vast a generalization? For as we all know, generalization tends to slip into abstraction; and abstraction, while it is useful for many things from Hegelian philosophy to Vice-Chancellors' speeches, is not the language of the arts.

Now the check on effusion, the necessary constraint exerted on the spate of emotion, can be applied in the work of art by certain devices or contrivances, and of these some form of *contrast* contrived within the make of the work is the device most favoured by the poets. Baudelaire employs more than one mode of contrast integrated in this way. His most effective check is the application of *irony* to the treatment of the pathetic theme. His observation is acute almost to the point of cruelty, 'merciless with the utmost sensibility', said Proust.[1] He sees what is grotesque or hideous in the condition of the afflicted. But he presents these aspects in the poem in a way that increases our commiseration without drawing our attention *directly* to the pathos or the suffering of the victim. 'Quelles bizarreries,' he exclaims elsewhere, 'ne trouve-t-on pas dans une grande ville, quand on sait se promener et regarder? La vie fourmille de monstres innocents.'[2]

Irony has been used effectively by most of the great poets and by many lesser ones. But if one were asked for examples from nineteenth-century poetry, I doubt whether more impressive ones could be found than in the other two poems in this trilogy. Here comes the fantastic figure of the first of the Seven Old Men suddenly intercepted through a breach in the fog: he is seen hobbling along leaning heavily on his staff with the 'turn' and gait

> D'un quadrupède infirme ou d'un juif à trois pattes.

And as for the little old women, their shrunken bodies when they die could be placed in a child's coffin:

> Avez-vous observé que maints cercueils de vieilles
> Sont presque aussi petits que celui d'un enfant?

Irony, I admit, is not exhibited in *Le Cygne*. The element here that corrects excess of feeling and eases the tension only to bring out the strength and depth of compassion by contrast, is an alternative tone that is almost anti-poetical, and for which I can find no single name. 'Bathos' would hardly do because the tone is deliberately contrived: it is not a defect

---

[1] See the remarkable comments on these poems in Proust's essay, 'Sainte-Beuve et Baudelaire' in *Contre Sainte-Beuve*.
[2] *Mademoiselle Bistouri* (*Petits Poèmes en prose*).

but an effect. Not to beat about the bush looking for a definition, I will simply refer to the colloquial tone of certain stanzas, or the ruminating manner as of a person talking to himself, the casual references to commonplace incidents, of which the chief—that of the swan—is recounted anecdotically. And it is the way these unemphatic allusions and incidental reminiscences, interjected with a touch of nonchalance, are contrasted with the resonant, elevated stanzas and their noble classical themes that constitutes the originality of this poem. The device of alternating a lower and a higher register has been so much used since Baudelaire's time (but without acknowledgements to him) that I am tempted to claim this poem as a major discovery in modern technique.

Let us see how it works.

In Part One the strongest note is struck in the first stanza, lamenting Andromache in exile as Virgil represents her in the third book of the *Aeneid*. In the second stanza the tone drops to a conversational level with an off-hand allusion to changes in the Parisian scene as the result of structural alterations in the neighbourhood of the Louvre. Note the realistic references to *la voirie*, etc.: road-making and the hurricane of work in progress.[1]

For Baudelaire the vital association with the exiled Andromache is not the reference in Virgil but the memory of a swan which, having broken loose from a menagerie

[1] In an earlier form of the verse the epithet to *ouragan* was *sale*. This has suggested to me that the meaning of *la voirie* might include 'scavenging'. People who went to Paris as far back as I did could doubtless recall the din the scavengers would make, invading the courtyard of old tenements at or before dawn and, after fulfilling their horribly noisy functions, disappearing through the *porte cochère* as they might through the backdoor of Hades. But perhaps it would put a strain even on the audacity of Baudelaire to thrust such operations almost into the presence of Andromache.

K

encamped near the Louvre, could find no water, and raised its head to heaven, longing for rain. Thereupon, after five stanzas at lower tension, the level rises to another classical reference:

> Vers le ciel quelquefois, comme l'homme d'Ovide,
> Vers le ciel ironique et cruellement bleu . . .

Ovid (*Metamorphoses*, book 1, ll. 85-6) distinguishes man from the animals in that he stands upright and lifts his brow to heaven. Baudelaire compares the gesture of his thirsty swan to that of Ovid's man; but the swan lifts its head to the blue sky in vain.

In the Second Part the tone of the first two stanzas could hardly be called colloquial, but it is low-pitched, quietly communicative, unemphatic and reminiscent. Suddenly it leaps to the highest point of indirect commiseration in the whole poem. Another classically inspired quatrain recalls Andromache's misfortune and the humiliations of her exile. And now appears what is perhaps the most skilful device of all: the gradual descent, an effectively managed diminuendo, a real 'dying fall'; the tone becoming plangently reflective and fading away into the most casual phrase in the poem. One wonders whether a good poem has ever finished so effectively on so feeble a note—*à bien d'autres encor!*

Here then we have unusual extremes of contrasted tones and levels of intensity, placed abruptly in juxtaposition, without transition, all within a sequence of thirteen stanzas. Yet the poem is a unit and its form will repay further study.

This arrangement of diverse tonal and structural elements is held together by a network of repetitive devices—resumptions, cross-references and interwoven motifs—which we must now examine. An example of the way the unity of the piece is maintained by picking up the same key words may be given at once. Note the reappearance of the phrase, 'Je pense à vous' (line 1) as 'Je pense à mon grand cygne' (Part ii, l. 6); and again, 'Je pense à la négresse' (last stanza but one), and finally 'Je pense aux matelots' (last line but one).

These reminders of the meditative mood of the poem are but superficial pointers to its form. The poem is based, formally, on a subtle interweaving of *themes* ('nuggets of meaning'), the chief of which are not difficult to unravel.

The important thing to realize about the thought structure of the poem is that it is not logical. That is, it is not based on the logical development of an argument or of an image, as in the well-known sonnet, *L'Albatros*. The formal originality of *Le Cygne* is that it approximates to the pattern of modern musical composition as exemplified in the movements of a symphony or a sonata. In sonata form, you will remember, distinctive or contrasted themes are developed, alternated or interwoven, usually to be worked out to a resolution. This can be contrasted with the form of a song or of a litany, in which you recognize from the first a fixed pattern of melody which repeats itself normally from the beginning to the end.

Baudelaire combined the achievement of an original art critic with a degree of intelligent interest in contemporary music which was exceptional among French poets of his generation. Among cultivated Frenchmen he was one of Wagner's earliest admirers.[1] He wrote a prose poem on Liszt and he reveals something of a connoisseur's reactions to Beethoven. I cannot here trace the connections in detail but I think we may assume that the poem we are studying

[1] See L. J. Austin, *L'Univers poétique de Baudelaire*, pp. 259–81; and note the phrase: 'Tout insuffisante que fut cette expérience, elle permit néanmoins à Baudelaire de pressentir, dans les *leit-motive*, "des intentions mystérieuses"' (p. 267). I return to the points here mentioned, at the end of the next chapter.

is related to the form developed by Beethoven, Liszt and Wagner at least in some of its structural aspects.

In *Le Cygne* we find the two dominant themes which the comparison with sonata form would lead us to expect: (1) the theme of Exile which is strongly announced in the first stanza by an evocation of Andromache in captivity; (2) the theme of the changing metropolis: 'Le vieux Paris n'est plus' . . .

The first theme appears to be dropped as abruptly as it is presented. It reappears, however, in the episode of the swan which has escaped but cannot find water and is still, therefore, alienated from its native element. It reappears once more in the episode of the negress who suffers from the hostile climate of the north (ii, 5). And it continues to resound with fainter and fainter echoes, but with broader implications, in the skilfully managed diminuendo to die away, softly but distinctly, like a premonition of the role of the 'petite phrase' in Proust.

I am assuming, as model, a form of musical composition which is not characterized by common logic. If I might adopt the words 'musical illogicality', then I could point to a minor example of it in the change of order between the mention of Andromache and that of the swan in each part. In Part One the thought of Andromache in exile leads to a fertilization of the poet's memory, in which the episode of the swan constitutes the second statement of the theme of exile. Whereas in Part Two the poet says,

> Je pense à mon grand cygne . . .
> . . . et puis à vous,
> Andromaque . . .

This, in strict logic, is a contradiction in order. But modern music does not require that the order in which the themes or motifs recur should remain the same. On the contrary we should find such rigorous repetition monotonous and wearisome, and should *expect* the order to be changed and re-created by the composer in accordance with his own free intuition. All music is not written in a recurrent pattern like 'God save the Queen', and less and less poetry has been written in this way since Baudelaire.

The same holds for the second theme, that of the changing metropolis. 'Paris change' (first stanza of Part Two) recovers the motif of 'Le vieux Paris n'est plus' of Part One (second stanza, l. 3) and so on. I need not repeat what we have just examined under the variations of tone. But I should like in conclusion to warn against a defect inevitable in all methods of analysis applied to works of literature and art.

Analysis is a process of intellectual scrutiny, the danger of which is that it separates things out too much, whereas the variations of tone and of form to which we have been attending belong to the very make or *facture* of the poem and together constitute its formal originality. I hope you will still feel that *Le Cygne* is a well integrated poem, and I wish I had the space and the skill to discuss it as a synthesis. There is room for only one suggestion more and as this one is entirely personal, I will risk it with a word of caution to young readers and an apology to their distinguished elders. In words that are all too simple, I suggest that the unity of this poem comes from an underlying sense of *loss*. The exiles have lost their homelands and the poet is losing the familiar landmarks of the city that has been his home. But such is the incantatory skill of the poem that, for me, these are symbols of a sense of loss similar to that felt to be suggested by parts of Proust's work. Recently Miss Rebecca West pointed out that the English translation of the title as 'The Recovery of Time Past' misses the significance of the original, *A la Recherche du Temps perdu*. *Perdu* suggests the irrevocable, the irretrievable, what is beyond redemption, at least by conscious or voluntary effort. There is some hint of exile from Eden that links Proust's work to Baudelaire's. But we cannot pursue that obscure hint here.

At the last moment, however, you may well ask, what of that other poem to the Lost which both Mallarmé and Swinburne were fond of—*Les Litanies de Satan*, from the brief subsection of *Les Fleurs du Mal* called *Révolte*? In it, you will remember, Satan is presented as the supreme Exile, the Comforter and Consoler of all the other lost souls.

Well, despite its celebrated patronage, the only interest I find this poem has from the standpoint of our discussion of *Le Cygne*, is one of complete contrast. The exiles attain a kind of *paradis artificiel* and their reunion is chanted in verses based rigorously and sacriligiously on the *litany* of the Church service. In exact terms the form of this poem is bound to a repetitive device, and is not, as in *Le Cygne*, a free creation.

Of much greater interest to us is the fine sonnet, *La Mort des Pauvres*. Not long ago it was pronounced a masterpiece by Jean Prévost in one of the most perceptive books ever written on Baudelaire. It is a curious fact that both Baudelaire and Proust, deep pessimists though they were, have yet a mysterious appreciation of death, as if they felt that in some obscure way it might disclose secret assurances of immortality. Death, in *La Mort des Pauvres*, is more than the 'Libérateur céleste' of Lamartine's faded apostrophe: it is the exultant fulfilment of all the ideals denied in life to the destitute and the disinherited. As if, far off at the end of the journey, all exiles find a welcome conforming in spirit to what Jean Prévost effectively called 'la charité de Baudelaire'—Baudelaire's charity, which is, I suggest, only another word for the commiseration, indirectly but finely expressed in the poem I have tried to discuss here.

IX

LAFORGUE'S 'VERS LIBRE' AND THE FORM OF 'THE WASTE LAND'

JULES LAFORGUE (1860–87) was born of French parents at Montevideo (Uruguay). Most of his childhood was spent at Tarbes, Gautier's birthplace, within sight of the Pyrenees. In 1876 Laforgue came to Paris, which he left five years later for Berlin to take up the post of reader to the Empress Augusta. Returning to Paris in 1886, he married a young Englishwoman, Miss Leah Lee, but he died of consumption in the following year. The tone and detail of his work give indirect hints of the tragic effect of the malady from which he had suffered for some time. But it is a point in his favour that Laforgue never bemoans his fate in the way the romantic poets lament their misfortunes. They could indulge in plangent self-pity, whereas he mocks at his sufferings and prefers objective allusion to confession.

The distinguishing feature of Laforgue's work in prose as well as verse is a particular kind of humorous fantasy which is easier to detect than to define. His humour has a wry touch of sadness—the phrase, 'un sourire navré', hits it off well—which may often seem too cleverly expressed to be frankly either sad or comic. In all he wrote tender feeling and acute sensibility are held in check by a constant play of irony, often indulged in at his own expense. To express this complex mood Laforgue invented a form of verbal buffoonery which he called 'clownesque'. His work helped to give vogue to the introspective pierrots and to the parodies of Hamlet that kept reappearing in French and English poetry for many years after his death.

Today the form of some of Laforgue's last poems is found to be more interesting than the spirit of his work. He stated that the 'type' he aimed at was realized in 'the piece about the Winter', that is *L'Hiver qui vient*, which appeared first in the Symbolist review, *La Vogue*, for 16 August 1886. What he intended to discard in inventing this form is described in a letter to a friend: 'J'oublie de rimer, j'oublie le nombre de syllabes, j'oublie la distinction de strophes', and he insisted that the verses of this new kind of poem should all begin at the margin, aligned like prose.

These claims represent Laforgue's *ideal* of freedom. Actually, the freest of his poems show marked vestiges of the traditional versification. Rhyme, regular or irregular, is the rule rather than the exception in *L'Hiver qui vient*,[1] while lines that are indistinguishable from alexandrines occur in the second paragraph and elsewhere. But the regular strophe or stanza-form has been abandoned, and lines of various length are grouped in paragraphs according to the sense of the poet's thought or the impulse of his feeling. The great innovation is to have rejected the count of syllables on which French versification had been based for centuries, and to have substituted a free rhythmical movement which no longer obeys a preconceived or preselected metrical standard.

Looked at literally, and with the title in mind, *L'Hiver qui vient* has for theme the coming of the first winter storms and

[1] The poem is fully rhymed except for three line-endings which have assonance: *s'amène* with *chemine* and *vertes* with *mortes*, which however rhymes with *portes*. In a few cases the rhyming is internal: *usines*, l. 6, rhymes with *bruines* above, and *personne*, l. 31, rhymes with *frisonne* in the same line. Actually the rhymes play a big role in marking the rhythms and in closing the phrases and paragraphs, while they help to maintain the tone by the repetition of sounds and echoes.

the poet's lamentation that they should bring the autumn to an end. This poetic commonplace is treated in a bantering manner with much fantasy in the images and with a new range of rhythmical movement. The poem might at first appear to be a parody of romantic feeling as inspired by the season of falling leaves, high winds, and the melancholy mood of lovers for whom the rustic benches will soon be too damp to sit on. But it is not so simple as that. The poem is certainly a parody of romantic language, but behind this Laforgue is mocking his own very sensitive feelings. He is treating them to strong doses of his playful but poignant irony.

The surface meaning is given in the first phrase: 'Blocus sentimental'. Impending winter, rain, wind and early nightfall 'blocade', that is, frustrate the conventional emotions we associate with Autumn. Then, with typical incongruity and to reassert the clowning mood, the author throws in the name of a well-known shipping company that trades with the Near East: 'Messageries du Levant.' This conveniently provides a rhyme with 'vent'.

This passage, and still less the poem as a whole, could not be called witty. Its language has nothing of the hard sparkle of the French social *esprit*. Nor could it be called 'light verse'; its underlying mood is the reverse of levity. Its originality (after that of the language of Tristan Corbière) depends much on the introduction—one might almost say the 'injection'—of jargon into a medium which had been used too long for eloquent effects. Laforgue brings his counter-effects off, partly by inserting clichés from common speech and slang. Tnis device, which he must have seen exemplified in Corbière's *Amours jaunes* (1873), Laforgue has passed on to poets ranging from those of his time to ours. And with the clichés come frequent play on word meanings, punning on various shades of synonyms, ambiguities beloved of the modern muse, and parody, a delightful example of which appears in the next paragraph:

> On ne peut plus s'asseoir: tous les bancs sont mouillés...

This is Banville's little poem transcribed in colloquial language. Banville himself had taken his theme from a popular *chanson*. The mingling of the traditional and cultural with the contemporary and colloquial is highly characteristic of Laforgue and of many of his successors.

Soleils plénipotentiaires, etc. Here the bantering tone induces an extravagant spate of images, a kind of word-play involving picturesque phrases, an occasional learned or literary reference and a childish fiction or two—the whole amalgam rapidly moving in a pseudo-poetic sequence making more sound than sense. The word *Pactoles*, from Pactolus, a river in Asia Minor, the sands of which were said to be laden with gold, suggests sunlight. And so, by free association, the summer suns are addressed in a mock-romantic manner, as fully empowered to preside over the lucrative transactions of agricultural shows—but where are they now buried? In abrupt contrast the pallid winter sun is evoked in a series of maladive similes, some of them of a startling realism. The horns and cries of the hunt have tried to bring the moribund sun back to life, but in vain!

> Et il gît là, comme une glande arrachée dans un cou,
> Et il frissonne, sans personne!...

In clinical audacity this forestalls the simile that fluttered the Georgian dovecotes when *The Love Song of J. Alfred Prufrock* appeared:

> When the evening is spread out against the sky
> Like a patient etherised upon a table...

Oh! leurs ornières des chars de l'autre mois, etc. Hugo, who wrote the line:

> Les grands chars gémissants qui reviennent le soir,

was not the only French poet before Laforgue who referred to wagons returning through the woods. A more pertinent example is found in one of the two *vers libre* poems written by Rimbaud, which suggests a close parallel in imagery:

> Les chars d'argent et de cuivre . . .
> Les courants de la lande,
> Et les ornières immenses du reflux,
> Filent circulairement vers l'est . . .[1]

Such examples may have prompted Laforgue's fantasia on the word *ornières*. But of greater interest here are the examples of the mental phenomenon to which we have referred as 'free association'. By this a word, a phrase or an image prompts others to follow in spontaneous succession without any apparent reason or logical connection. Here Laforgue's phrases develop through a bewildering series of mixed and disconnected metaphors. The ruts made by the carts in the moist soil are thought of as 'rails', rising in the mock-heroic manner of Don Quixote (who tilted at sheep as well as at windmills) towards the patrols of the clouds which the wind drives in rout across the sea to sheepfolds on the other side of the Atlantic.

Adieu vendanges, et adieu tous les paniers. The *paniers* are, literally, the baskets in which the ripe grapes are gathered. But through a device of which Laforgue is fond, a different sense of the word supervenes, namely the 'panniers' or 'hoops' in

---

[1] *Marine*. A still more striking resemblance (apart from the rhythm) will be found in Rimbaud's prose poem actually called *Ornières*: 'les mille rapides ornières de la route humide. Défilé de féeries. En effet: des chars . . .'

ladies skirts as painted for instance by Watteau (1694-1721). The *bourrées* are old-fashioned dances his figures might have engaged in under the chestnut trees. Then, without transition, an abrupt, realistic contrast is introduced, recalling the ailments brought on by the cold season; they include the one from which Laforgue died.

I will conclude this chapter with some indications of the influence which I believe the general shape of this piece, along with some prominent features of its technique, exerted on the writing of *vers libre* poems subsequently. Two cases that it would be interesting to compare with this example are the *vers libre* poems of Emile Verhaeren, who was one of the most prolific writers of them in the generation after Laforgue's death,[1] and Mr Eliot's poem, *The Waste Land*, which appeared in 1922. We have space only for a few brief observations.

L'Hiver qui vient was written at the time of, or soon after, Laforgue's discovery of Whitman's *Leaves of Grass*. Some line for line translations by him of a few of Whitman's poems had already appeared in *La Vogue* for 18 June 1886. But in his own free verse he was far from going to the full length of imitating Whitman's 'lawless line'. An obvious difference is that, as we have said, Laforgue's technique depends much on effects of rhyming, a habit which, in the letter to his friend, he said he had abandoned. Of Verhaeren's free verse persistent rhyming is a marked characteristic; but it is not of Mr Eliot's. With a few irregularities the lines of his early poem, *Prufrock*, rhyme throughout. But in *The Waste Land* rhymes are infrequent, occurring usually at the end of parts or of paragraphs.

Let us glance a little more closely at the shape of

[1] Verhaeren, who was five years older than Laforgue, did not begin to publish poems in *vers libre* until 1888-9.

Laforgue's poem. In place of a traditional arrangement of metrical stanzas or paragraphs of alexandrines *à rimes plates*, we find groups of lines irregular in number and varying in length. The length of each line depends on its meaning or on the rhythmical impulse that produced it. This develops in a way similar to that of sonata form. The first line or the initial group of lines announces the dominant theme or, as the musicians say, the 'subject'. And the theme is developed, dropped, resumed and interwoven with another or others, and there are recurrences and repetitions of words and phrases, though not in regular order. As a result of this spontaneous treatment the lines fall naturally into paragraphs of unpremeditated length.

It is a curious comment on the quest for freedom of form, so ardent in France towards the end of the nineteenth century, that, no sooner had the new mode become popular than most of those who began to cultivate it tended to adopt a pattern that was clearly differentiated by its practitioners, although it offered considerable scope for variation. Immediately following Laforgue one of the most assiduous writers of *vers libre* was, as we have said, the Flemish poet of French expression, Emile Verhaeren. His devotion to the form was such that much of his verse seems now, not only to have conformed to the pattern, but to have confirmed and extended it. Verhaeren remains the most persistent and versatile practitioner of the Laforguian model.

A close study of *tempo* and *tone* would show how near in other ways some of Verhaeren's poems are to this model. Few traits characterize the new form more clearly than its ability to give impressions of movement, speed, strain and urgency:

Accélérons, accélérons, c'est la saison bien connue, cette fois. . . .

This impression, blended with the full range of sonorous effects, especially the strident, high-pitched tones to which Laforgue, in the course of his poem actually calls attention, emphasizes the potentials of the pattern. They are exploited to the point of paroxysm in a poem of Verhaeren's in which the tempestuous wailings and laments of *L'Hiver qui vient* are amplified and accelerated into the swiftly moving insurrectional rhythms of *La Révolte* from *Les Villes tentaculaires* (1895), a poem, it must be said, quite beyond the capabilities of Laforgue's ingenious talents.

And there is one more comparison worth making. The tone of elation and of emphasis *pitched in the Vocative* suggests a kind of ode. Laforgue has written an ironic Ode to Winter, inspired by lamentations verging on exasperation but saved from sentimentality by outbursts of self-parodying expostulation. 'La saison' as Laforgue calls it—with its attributes of wind, rain and whirling leaves, echoes of the hunting horn, coughs in the dormitories, colds in the head,

> Et toute la misère des grands centres—

is addressed on a note of mocking complaint, 'cette note' which he proposes to 'give' each year and which rings throughout the poem. I think it could be said that Laforgue created the Ode in *vers libre* and that Verhaeren helped to perpetuate it in many strenuous or tender forms. How close his imitation, or reminiscence, of details could be will appear from a couple of examples. First a few lines from Laforgue's poem:

> C'est la saison, c'est la saison, la rouille envahit les masses,
> La rouille ronge en leurs spleens kilométriques
> Les fils télégraphiques des grandes routes où nul ne passe.
>
> Les cors, les cors, les cors—mélancoliques! . . .
> Mélancoliques!

S'en vont, changeant de ton,
Changeant de ton et de musique,
Ton ton, ton taine, ton ton! . . .
Les cors, les cors, les cors! . . .
S'en sont allés au vent du Nord.

Now a few from Verhaeren's *Les Campagnes hallucinées*, published seven years later:

>Les gens d'ici n'ont rien de rien,
>Rien devant eux
>Que l'infini, ce soir, de la grand'route.
>
>Chacun porte au bout d'une gaule,
>En un mouchoir à carreaux bleus,
>Chacun porte dans un mouchoir,
>Changeant de main, changeant d'épaule,
>Chacun porte
>Le linge usé de son espoir.
>
>Les gens s'en vont, les gens d'ici,
>Par la grand'route à l'infini.

A lapse of thirty-six years separates the appearance of Laforgue's poem from that of *The Waste Land*. Mr Eliot's admission of having come across Laforgue in 1908–9 is known to everyone interested in his work. But evidence seems quite insufficient to suggest a debt to *L'Hiver qui vient* in any sense comparable to that shown in the early pastiche, *Conversation galante*. Influences however can be indirect, circumlocutory or subterranean in their ramifications; they can proceed from an *ambiance* made up of attitudes of mind and tentative experiments which project hints and intimations from a phase of literary and artistic activity or even from a period of discussion in the past. Even then it may be wiser to indulge one's taste for comparisons than to speculate on the chances of direct or indirect effects.

I confess I cannot open *The Waste Land* without thinking of Laforgue's 'piece about the Winter' even though, as 'The Burial of the Dead' develops, all grounds for comparison vanish. Each of the two poems begins by lamenting the advent of a season, though the tone of reproach is rumbustious in the one case and restrained in the other. The opening bars, tuned to their different keys, run on in each case for about half a dozen lines. Then, without transition, a new tempo supervenes, a different rhythm, while in each case the dominant seasonal theme is being developed in different terms: in the one through parody of an old song, in the other through light conversation heard in showery weather. The two *contents* are different in nature and in tone, but the function of the sudden change appears to be the same. A mode of progression by juxtaposition has been established in Laforgue's poem tentatively, in Mr Eliot's with assurance.

Neither of these *motifs*, however, the damp seats in the autumn woods or the surprise of summer

> coming over the Starnbergersee
> With a shower of rain . . .

is developed far. After a few lines comes another break. This time Laforgue's new movement is much the more diversified and rapid, but it expands and contracts in a wild cadenza of fanciful and fatalistic images. At the corresponding point in *The Waste Land* the summer voices cease and there is a brief pause. Then comes what is for me the deepest and most resonant note in modern poetry, the note that made us, long ago, think as well as feel. It struck the death knell of Georgian poetry as now, for me, it eclipses Laforgue. 'By 1912,' says Mr Hugh Kenner, 'the Laforguian lode was worked out.' Yet much remains to be said about the art of discontinuous composition which Laforgue had practised lightly but which projects

> What are the roots that clutch...

with such arresting force.

The 'sudden wrenching juxtapositions' which, in his excellent book on the poetry of T. S. Eliot,[1] Mr Kenner finds characteristic of *The Waste Land* are vastly more abrupt than the 'shifts of tone' he finds in Laforgue. But, to borrow a phrase from *L'Hiver qui vient*, Laforgue's modest breaks and fresh starts may have helped to 'give the note'. This, however, would not be worth suggesting, did not all these matters of disruption and alternation of theme, tone and tempo lead back to a much wider context of experiment.

Discussing the lay-out of *The Waste Land* Mr Kenner speaks of 'that form, originally an accident produced by Pound's cutting'.[2] And again, a trifle more tentatively, referring to the author of the poem: 'He was credited with having created a new mode of poetic organization, as he had, though specific instances of the cinematic effect were as likely as not attributable to Pound's cutting.'[3] With the specific instances of Mr Pound's 'surgical operation' I am not concerned here. But the implication that it achieved so much looks to me like a contradiction in terms. Could a major invention by one poet be due to the scissors of another? Was there not, rather, a well-informed connivance behind the deed? And was it not part of the originality of the partners in 'compromise' to have recognized the one original movement in the poetry of their time and to have *studied* it, as Mr Kenner himself affirms they did?[4]

[1] Hugh Kenner, *T. S. Eliot, The Invisible Poet*, W. H. Allen, 1960.
[2] P. 260.   [3] P. 156.
[4] 'His form was drawn from the *study* of the models, not their imitation'.... Op. cit., p. 12.

Mr Eliot came across Laforgue in 1908-9, and if I may add a morsel of evidence, I remember being advised to consult Mr Pound as 'the man' who could enlighten me on what I wanted to know about the *vers libre* in 1913. His advice was characteristically generous and practical: he provided addresses of *verslibristes* in Paris with whom he had recently talked. Clearly the sources and channels of the techniques of modern verse had been tapped by the most percipient poets then domiciled in England a decade and a half before *The Waste Land* appeared.

Beyond Eliot and Pound, behind the *verslibristes* stands a poet whose status has continuously risen and whose influence is now sensed rather than seen (no one has attempted the statistics involved) to have been enormous. Baudelaire, it is true (as Rimbaud complained), had been content to adapt the traditional versification to his own devices. But the variations in tone and rhythm which we indicated when glancing at *Le Cygne* show examples of a mode of composition checked by suspensions and revived by resumptions, with shifting levels of language ranging from Racinian diction to casual asides which—we would contend—founded a tradition of suppressed transitional technique that passed directly, or it may have been through Laforgue, to the later poets.

Just one more point of prior interest. When Mr Kenner speaks of 'thematic links between section and section', he is using musical language. Of *Prufrock* he says, 'it progresses from theme to theme by discontinuous means, as in the *Waste Land*.'[1] Then comes the cue I want: 'The opulent Wagnerian pathos with its harmonic rather than linear development and its trick of entrancing the attention with *leitmotifs* is never unrelated to the methods of *The Waste Land*.'[2] Nor, I suggest, was it unrelated to the method of Baudelaire's poem, *Le Cygne*.

[1] P. 211.   [2] P. 146.

This poem which appeared in 1860 was collected in a new edition of *Les Fleurs du Mal* that Baudelaire saw through the press in 1861. In that year had appeared his article on *Richard Wagner et Tannhäuser*. This shows its author's familiarity with the basic structure and novelty of the Wagnerian opera: 'Tannhäuser représente la lutte des deux principes', etc.[1] But it is in the passages quoted from Liszt or Wagner himself that we seize Baudelaire's perception of the radical distinctions and of the primitive model of the union of poetry and music—'la combinaison profondément réfléchie, étonnamment habile et poétiquement intelligente, avec laquelle Wagner, *au moyen de plusieurs phrases principales*, a serré *un nœud mélodique* qui constitue tout son drame'.[2]

The phrase is Liszt's. He is emphasizing the combination of contrasted themes in the ultimate resolution of the Wagnerian dramatic conflict.

A great distance separates the last chord of *Tannhäuser*, or even of *Parsifal*, from the word for Peace on which *The Waste Land* ends. But at intervals between, it may not seem inconsequent to have listened with Baudelaire as

Un vieux Souvenir sonne à plein souffle du cor!

or quite irrelevant to pick up Laforgue's last line again:

J'essaierai en chœur d'en donner la note.

---

[1] La Pléiade edition, p. 1060.
[2] Ibid., p. 1068 (the italics may be Baudelaire's).

X

VERLAINE AND RIMBAUD

THE life of Verlaine is not of sufficient interest in itself to deserve detailed attention here. It is actually the tragedy of an exceptionally gifted but weak-willed man who might appear to have squandered his talents in the course of a long degeneration, had not his genius won wide recognition even before he died in 1896. Since then the popular reception of his poems has greatly increased, though they have recently lost some of the attraction they had for the best critical taste. We could not call Verlaine an autobiographical poet. But, as many of his most distinctive lyrics turn on incidents in his own experience or catch subtle echoes of his moods of delight, foreboding or remorse, a few relevant facts from his biography may help us to appreciate how some of his best-known poems came to be written, among them those that are almost too fragile to annotate by direct comment.

Paul Verlaine was born in the garrison town of Metz on 30 March 1844. His father, a French army officer, retired in 1851 and came to live in Paris. The boy was sent to the Lycée Bonaparte and took his *baccalauréat* in 1862. Two years later he obtained a clerkship at the Hôtel de Ville; but he neglected his duties in favour of writing verse and discussing poetry with friends as they loafed about town.

In 1866 his first collection appeared. It was called *Poèmes saturniens* and, though praised by Anatole France, it attracted no serious attention. Most of these pieces conform to the reigning Parnassian manner, the question,

> Est-elle en marbre ou non: la Vénus de Milo?

implying that verse must be firm and smoothly sinuous like statuary. But a few of the shorter poems are of a novel and experimental type. Of these the *Chanson d'Automne* has become one of the best known short lyrics of the nineteenth century. So familiar in fact that its opening lines were used to announce the invasion of Northern France by the allied forces on D-day 1944. Brief, simple but poignant, this little song reveals a mastery of poetic melody which was unique in a school where rhythms were chiselled rather than intoned.

In 1869 Verlaine produced *Les Fêtes galantes*, his masterpiece according to those critics who prefer it to the later, more miscellaneous collection, *Sagesse*. The immediate inspiration of the new series was the appearance of a book by the Goncourts on French art in the eighteenth century. This study revived interest in the refined, voluptuous paintings of idyllic scenes in idealized natural settings by Watteau, Lancret, Fragonard, Boucher and lesser masters of the *manière galante*.

With the *beau monde* in beautiful dresses and graceful attitudes were blended figures and costumes from the Commedia dell'Arte. Harlequin, Pierrot, Scapin and Scaramouche seem to step down from the trestles, to flit in and out of Verlaine's *fêtes* and, after the masque is over, to haunt French poetry off and on for the rest of the century.

A point of fine distinction arises here: Professor Antoine Adam, who has written a book for students on Verlaine, suggests that the tone of this 'poetic and *galant*' tradition in painting is bright, sunlit and joyous, and that it was the Goncourts who in the mid-nineteenth century interpreted it as melancholic.

Here, on the other hand, is what Mr Michael Ayrton said in discussing Watteau's painting, *The Music Party*, in a broadcast:

Watteau was one of those artists naturally given to nostalgia. To him, one suspects, a golden age—an age of Rubens, of Titian's Bacchanals, of the fiery loves of gods with mortals—lived on as in a dream, silver, not golden:

> Dans le vieux parc solitaire et glacé
> Deux spectres ont évoqué le passé,

as Paul Verlaine, re-evoking Watteau in his turn, saw and celebrated the silver age, then past. Yet they are not spectres...[1]

Which is the correct impression? From my limited knowledge of the rococo style, I have no right to bias your decision. Otherwise I must agree with Professor Adam when he says of the Goncourts' study of 1860: 'elle met l'accent sur le côté mélancolique et lunaire, et laisse moins discerner sa joie, sa clarté, son élan vers le bonheur'.

In 1870 Verlaine married Mlle Mauté de Fleurville, half-sister of the composer, Charles de Sivry. The engagement and the anticipation of the event provided one of his purest sources of inspiration, and his feelings were reflected in a small collection called *La Bonne Chanson*, which was announced that year. Owing to the outbreak of the Franco-Prussian war publication was postponed for two years. The invasion of France was naturally a disturbing event and the Commune of the next year was even more menacing. Trapped in the beleaguered capital, the Verlaine ménage feared implication in the civil dissensions and decided to escape to the north of France. But by now the poet's unstable temperament and shifty character are out of control. His life, which has for long been fluctuating between decency, dis-

---

[1] *The Listener.* 14 July, 1960. Quoted by permission of the author and of the editor.

traction and despondency, shows definite signs of those degenerate habits which will drag him down until, long after his dissipations have crippled him physically they begin to impair the quality of his work, and ruin his later output. Fortunately this catastrophe is a long way off: periods of elation and of regeneration are still in front of him, although by now his married life is almost destroyed. A mysterious poetic genius, far stronger than his own, has swung into his ken, disrupted all prospects of domestic happiness and put an abrupt end to the 'bonne chanson'. Rimbaud has arrived.

From his mother's farm at Charleville, near the Belgian frontier, the boy-poet had previously communicated with his elder in Paris and had sent him some verses. Verlaine recognized exceptional gifts and, on receiving a second letter, wrote back: 'Venez, chère grande âme! on vous appelle, on vous attend.' Rimbaud tramps to Paris and sweeps Verlaine off his unsteady feet. But his uncouth appearance and arrogant manners disgust most of the people he meets and, after hanging on for a few months, he returns, disillusioned, to La Roche. In the following spring (1872) Rimbaud joins Verlaine again and persuades him to leave Paris and go off with him to Belgium and England.

The only good thing the two vagabonds do *not* leave behind is their genius and at odd moments—most probably under the influence of the younger man who was already an audacious innovator—Verlaine puts together the delicate little pieces which compose *Romances sans Paroles*. These were not published until 1874. But by then tragic events had happened. The marriage had been dissolved and Verlaine had spent several months in prison as the result of a bungled pistol-shot. He had quarrelled with Rimbaud and had wounded him in the forearm. One thinks with regret of the grip such trivial incidents have on our memories. Whereas the sole importance attaching to this incident is the fact that

Verlaine's sojourn in the prison of Mons, roughly within the years 1873-5, was a productive period. It was then he began to write some of the poems that went into the most famous of his collections, *Sagesse*, published in 1881.

Verlaine's term of imprisonment was shortened as a reward for good conduct, and he returned alone to England where he taught French in East Anglian grammar schools. By 1885 he was back in Paris, a sick man, broken in health and increasingly intemperate. But—such were the fluctuations of his destiny—it is now that his fame begins; he becomes the literary idol of the cafés of the *rive gauche*. Even the hospital ward to which he retired from time to time, is sought for as a Mecca by young aspirants and old admirers. Anatole France was one of the faithful. A phrase from an article he wrote about Verlaine has often been quoted: 'Il est inconscient; et c'est un poète comme il ne s'en rencontre pas un par siècle.'

But is Verlaine an 'unconscious' poet? His shortest lyrics might seem to suggest that he was. The truth, however, may be different. Verlaine was, at his best, a subtle and competent artist who had the notable gift of concealing his craft and not talking much about it. Anatole France was probably nearer the mark when, in one of his novels, he depicts the poet (under a pseudonym) seated before a glass of absinthe, scribbling verses on cigarette paper. The breeze whirls the paper in the air. But the sly fellow catches it before it has flown out of reach and carefully adjusts the new verse to his stock. That is probably more like the real Verlaine.

Where does he stand today as a poet and how can we characterize his work with a view to distinguishing it from Rimbaud's?

Well, our contemporary taste for extreme metaphysical subtleties has placed even his best work at a discount. Verlaine did not lack subtlety or intelligence. But he hadn't the kind of intellect or turn of wit that make the metaphysical. Yet I think it could be claimed that, for at least fifty years from the recognition of his significance in the early 80's of the last century, Verlaine was the most popular of modern French poets after Baudelaire; and to judge by the place given to him in anthologies, this may still be a true estimate. The non-academic literary critics, however, make few references to him today; though I think all would agree that the work of his best periods is likely to retain a place among the genuinely favoured varieties of the abundant flowering of lyrical genius in France during the latter half of the nineteenth century. A poet whom people read, but who has had no influence on the development of poetry since his day, seems to be Professor Adam's verdict.

Can we find reasons for Verlaine's popularity? His poetry is intimate but clear. Often subtle and genuinely refined, it is not the work of a 'poet-critic' and, as a phrase in his one theoretical poem declares, he disallows the use of wit. Although he lived through the heyday of Symbolist theorizing and experimentation, even when, in his *Art Poétique*, he balances advice and admonition, it is a song he sings; and what cannot be sublimated into song he rejects as conventional writing:

> Et tout le reste est littérature.

Only his conception of poetry as music brings him into line with the Symbolists. With their elaboration of the Symbol he has no patience. Although he shared the admiration felt by his contemporaries for Mallarmé, he could scoff at the 'school' that gathered solemnly around the Master and whom he called 'Les Cymbalistes'. Verlaine was in no sense an extremist. He encouraged the cult of music in preference to the plastic arts, yet even here—as we have seen—neither his taste nor his practice was exclusive: some of his best poems are more or less directly inspired by painting. To sum up, he was systematic in nothing, and all his work is readable at sight.

Broad discriminations are tolerable in such a discussion as this only when space is short, and that is my excuse for indulging in one or two more. I want to suggest that the interest we feel in Verlaine's best work is due to its being a poetry of the Sensibility, not of the Imagination. I risk the assumption that most readers have more sensibility than imagination, in the sense that most of us react more readily and more genuinely to a type of poetry that appeals to our feelings than we do to a type that demands a high degree of imaginative response. Or to consider concrete examples, it seems easier to be attracted to some of the slight but poignant poems of Verlaine—those dealing with situations we are familiar with in a style that has a certain charm of originality and freshness but which is not outside our range of instant comprehension—than it is to react fully to some of the vast frescoes and cosmic visions of Victor Hugo's pictorial manner.

Verlaine's sensibility is always human. It is extremely responsive to such moods and impressions as civilized people —men and women who have at least some cultivation—can and do at times experience, but which they could never perhaps express directly, except by using the smooth commonplaces and clichés of sentiment.

It is useful, I think, when discussing the art of Verlaine, to differentiate between the way he deals with impressions coming to him from outside, and moods arising from within. To illustrate I will refer to the examples given by Professor A. M. Boase in his *Anthology of Modern French Poetry*. Choosing instances from the *Poèmes saturniens*, Professor Boase says:
. . . an 'etching' such as the macabre *Effet de Nuit* recalling at once Callot and Goya, illustrates, in its economy of means, the point

of departure of a poetic impressionism which is one important aspect of Verlaine's future work. Another is to be found in the unmistakable musical cadences of *Mon Rêve familier* or the over-quoted *Chanson d'Automne*.

In *Effet de Nuit* the object that has inspired the poet is the work of an artist, Callot or Goya, or perhaps both: the little poem is therefore a *transposition d'art*. On the other hand, the musical cadences of *Mon Rêve familier* and the *Chanson d'Automne* originate in the poet's mind (prompted, I am tempted to suggest, by the 'repetends' of Edgar Allan Poe) and are inspired by his moods.

Professor Antoine Adam claims that Verlaine's impressionism comes from the painters. The Impressionist revolution was happening between 1870 and 1874, the year when their first Exhibition was held in Paris. A canvas exhibited by Monet, and called 'Impression' gave its name to the movement. The influence on Verlaine he sees at its best in a poem like *Walcourt*, which is composed entirely of nouns and adjectives without a single verb. It belongs to the series called *Paysages belges* in *Romances sans Paroles* and, according to M. Adam, it made Verlaine at that date 'le poète de l'Impressionnisme'.[1]

Verlaine's moods are not too clearly differentiated and are never defined. Their expression remains for the most part vague, hovering, as he recommended, between the indecisive and the precise. Never obscure in the way Mallarmé's poems are, Verlaine's reveries are given a touch of poignancy which makes them real, recognizable—and we have the relief of finding the inexpressible expressed. To use a cliché of the kind he would avoid, Verlaine has a special gift for touching

[1] M. Adam also points out that the reproaches that critics made to Verlaine are 'exactly' those that art critics now make against the Impressionist painters.

the tender chords of the heart. Not stirring the passions, but annotating the dream-side of experience, with its half-forgotten memories and haunting apprehensions. And these are our own as well as the poet's.

M. Octave Nadal, who has spoken finely of Verlaine, says that he can give us 'pure, direct sensation'. More often, I think, he communicates the vibrations and overtones of sensation rather than the shock itself. Distant things, faint colours, elegiac moods: all these are treated with an appearance of simplicity, immediacy, spontaneity and naturalness; and the economy of means employed to achieve these effects is astonishing. From his best verses we recognize those strange *états d'âme* when the mind is not fully occupied by a feeling, a sensation or a thought. Gently and discreetly they intimate what is on the borders of consciousness with a skill in the choice of words which, as Arthur Symons said, 'are sometimes words of the boudoir, sometimes words of the street'. What Verlaine reminds us of are the pleasanter things, it may be, but often they are tinged with melancholy or with foreboding, or chilled by a sudden sense of failure or remorse. In one of the most sensitive of his short poems Verlaine asks

> —Qu'as-tu fait, ô toi que voilà
> Pleurant sans cesse,
> Dis, qu'as-tu fait, toi que voilà,
> De ta jeunesse?

Professor Hackett, who speaks with authority on Rimbaud, contrasts, with this anxious question, the tone of a stanza by the latter:

> Oisive jeunesse
> A tout asservie,
> Par délicatesse
> J'ai perdu ma vie.

> Ah! Que le temps vienne
> Où les cœurs s'éprennent.

'Unlike Verlaine who ... *asks*,' says Professor Hackett, 'Rimbaud *affirms*: "J'ai perdu ma vie." Even in his most lyrical, child-like poems he is invariably unsentimental, alert, and self-critical.'[1]

This distinction could be made the basis for a prolonged discrimination between the two poets. But I shall have to be content with trying to indicate a few divergencies as clearly as possible. First, the temperaments and characters of the two men are diametrically opposed. Verlaine was essentially effeminate, self-indulgent and weak. Rimbaud was forceful to the point of violence, even of 'ferocity'—a word often used to suggest the extremes of his ardours and revulsions. He dominated others and, what is more in his favour, he could dominate himself. He produced far less than Verlaine in quantity, yet his extraordinary poetic gifts, applied within small compass, show a range of mood and of form almost equal to the variety we find in the voluminous productions of many a major poet.

Roughly but usefully we can divide Rimbaud's *œuvre*, as we have it, into three parts. First the juvenilia, the verses of a schoolboy of genius, whose astonishing talents one of his masters recognized and fostered. These early poems are more than imitations, much more than experiments in the manner of the Parnassians. Already some of them rival the best poems of their kind and time written in France. But soon the speed of the boy-poet's progress—which might today be compared with a rocket's—has left them far behind. This first phase may be said to end with a declaration of doctrine which Rimbaud sent, in the form of a couple of letters, one to his teacher, the second to a friend.

---

[1] C. A. Hackett, *Rimbaud*, Bowes and Bowes, p. 41.

'This letter,' says Professor Hackett, 'surely one of the most remarkable in any language, is in a limited sense a literary manifesto.'[1] It contained a phrase that has become famous: 'The Poet makes himself a *visionary* by a long, immense and reasoned *derangement* of *all the senses*.' And it was accompanied by a copy of *Le Bateau ivre*, which symbolizes a plunge into the unknown ocean of imaginative adventure—a complete breakaway from all past knowledge and experience. For all its violence, *Le Bateau ivre* is written in quatrains. But the quatrains are jostled with acceleration; their punctuation is disrupted or abandoned; and they seem ready to disintegrate with explosive imagery. Soon the forms Rimbaud will use break up altogether like the furious boat itself: the shreds of regular prosody yield to the free rhythms of poetic prose and the first real *vers libres* appear.

It was with these unprecedented liberties that Rimbaud was experimenting at the time when he was 'rockin' an' rol'n'' with Verlaine through Belgium and Southern England. And no doubt Verlaine saw many of these pieces in their original forms, noted their freedom and variety and discussed their technique with his companion. What became of them? The chronology of events at this stage has become a bone of contention. English authorities tend to support what may be called the older version, and I will do the same. The manuscript of *Les Illuminations* (Verlaine's name for Rimbaud's second flight of poems) seems to have been abandoned by him either to Verlaine or to another friend. He returned home to La Roche and wrote a new set of pieces in prose and verse, which he called *Une Saison en Enfer*. This corresponds to the third phase of his work and was more deliberately designed than the others. Rimbaud even persuaded his mother, a hard-headed, close-fisted *fermière*, to provide money for printing the collection. *Une Saison en Enfer* repre-

[1] Op. cit., p. 22.

sents Rimbaud's farewell to poetry and to the life he had lived so far. But no sooner were the pieces printed than he tried to destroy them, and he thought he had done so. Fortunately the printer had thrown a bundle of copies into a cellar. These were recovered after their author had deserted his tragic muse for ever.

Meanwhile the manuscript of the *Illuminations* seems to have circulated obscurely among some of Verlaine's contemporaries. In 1886 the poems were rescued and printed in a small review called *La Vogue*. Offprints were sold for a song, until gradually they began to attract attention and became, like copies of the review itself, *introuvables*.

I have already referred to the mixed nature of these poems: many in varieties of prose form, some in verse of diverse lengths and patterns, and one or two specimens of *vers libre*, probably the first deserving the name to be published. Some of the items are of the lightest texture and structure: their only rivals at that time being the short-line poems of Verlaine. And the question arises, which of the two poets influenced the other, or whether there was not an interchange of influences? Rimbaud was by far the more daring innovator, and it is usually considered that the liberties visible in *Romances sans Paroles*, which Verlaine was writing while they were together, show the impress and effect of the younger man's audacities. Professor Hackett does not stress the debt but he makes these judicious remarks about the relationship:

> Verlaine, in his article *Arthur Rimbaud* (in *Les Poètes maudits*) stressed the obvious quality of these poems—'le naïf, le très et l'exprès trop simple', a phrase that is very similar to his reference to the verse poems of the *Illuminations* as 'délicieusement faux exprès'. He also discerned, as might be expected, some of their main technical features—'assonances', 'mots vagues', 'phrases enfantines ou populaires'—for these were the devices he himself

had used in writing his most accomplished poems. What Verlaine failed to realize, however, was that these child-like lyrics represented a significant stage in Rimbaud's development. In them he is no longer the adolescent intoxicated with words; he is the poet, the *voyant*, in control of his material—which he is using in a new way.[1]

Let us ask ourselves in conclusion, what is the 'new way' in which Rimbaud writes poetry? A difficult question, because Rimbaud and his work are two aspects of one of the subtlest problems that modern literary psychology and the art of writing present us with; and an enormous amount of exegesis and commentary has already been expended in attempts to understand his personality and to explain it in relation to his poems. Our own attempt must rely on the commonplaces of admitted facts.

First as to the restricted area in which the poems of the two men appear to show resemblances, that is the type of naïve childlike inspiration that can produce lyricism which approximates to pure song. Note that these 'songs of innocence' are not common in any language, and that until Verlaine began to write there were few to be found in French. Fifty years ago those of us who passed from reading the songs of Shakespeare and lyrics like those of Shelley to modern French poetry—even to the shorter poems of the Romanticists—felt there was at least one note they never seemed to strike, and this we thought of as the ethereal note. What Verlaine referred to as 'la chose envolée' we had not then heard of—we students of 1910 for whom French poetry had catastrophically ended with the *Dies Irae* of Leconte de Lisle. The poets of France, as we knew them, never ceased to

---

[1] Op. cit., p. 47. See also Professor Hackett's further contribution to the problem in *Studies in Modern French Literature*, edited by L. J. Austin, Garnet Rees and E. Vinaver, Manchester University Press, 1961: 'Verlaine's influence on Rimbaud.'

be eloquent, and eloquence was precisely what Verlaine and Rimbaud were out to wring by the neck. Their ideal was to give poetry wings to fly.

With his part in this achievement Verlaine was content. After *Sagesse* his work declines and can drop to the level of mere scribbles sold by some of his harpies to complacent editors for a few *sous*. Rimbaud could be content with nothing on earth or above it. He towers over his discarded companion like Lucifer in perpetual revolt. Verlaine called him 'l'homme aux semelles de vent'; but this refers to the incessant wanderer. Rimbaud was much more than a wild man flitting from one place to another until he had found the hottest spot in Africa to try to make a fortune in. What we might call him today is the prototype of the 'homme révolté', the model of our angry young men, if only they knew it, at once an ancestor of the beat generation and a part-founder of Surrealism—except that he is by far the most gifted of all those who have sung the hymn of universal exasperation, tempered by visions of paradise regained on earth. Can there be any doubt that the variegated, haphazard, scintillating bits and pieces of verse and prose that he has left and whose exact reciprocity and significance are likely to remain in doubt, are but fragments of man's perpetual hymn of dissatisfaction with his experiences of time and sense, and of his hope for a future whose alluring novelties he cannot define? This, we may recall, was the burden of Baudelaire's poem *Le Voyage*; and as Baudelaire was the only poet whom Rimbaud acknowledged as his predecessor—and whom Verlaine began by imitating—it might seem appropriate to end with the last phrase of that famous apostrophe to Death:

> Nous voulons, tant ce feu nous brûle le cerveau,
> Plonger au fond du gouffre, Enfer ou Ciel, qu'importe?
> Au fond de l'Inconnu pour trouver du *nouveau*.

Yet even that won't do! We cannot rest with the thought of death in our minds when we say even a temporary farewell to Rimbaud. He had no interest in death.

Quoting those lovely lines from the *Bateau ivre*:

> Est-ce en ces nuits sans fond que tu dors et t'exiles,
> Million d'oiseaux d'or, ô future Vigueur,

M. Jean-Pierre Richard concludes:

Such is for Rimbaud the essential of poetic creation—to convert the nostalgia of Baudelaire into a movement of conquest; to transmute what has been into what is to come; to ignore as far as possible the present, and at every level of existence to awaken the *future Vigueur*.

XI

INTRODUCING
'DU CÔTÉ DE CHEZ SWANN'

A READER casting a cursory glance over the first volume of Proust's great work might be imagined to say: This is a kind of autobiography; the author is describing his past life in the first person and appears to be using paragraphs or passages resembling those found in personal diaries, based on detached memories of separate experiences. Many of the passages are long and some of them seem developed in 'essay' form as if they were meditations on the events described. Yet at first glance the work may appear to be episodic rather than continuous. And indeed as M. André Maurois has shown us, it is now found to have been composed basically from notes entered into *cahiers*, most of them to be rewritten and elaborated and finally fitted together or adapted to an appropriate place in the novel.

The *cahiers* were recently recovered from papers in the possession of Proust's descendants; and still more recently the manuscript of an earlier novel, completed but thrust aside as if it were a draft with which the author had grown dissatisfied, has come to light. This was published in 1952 under the title of *Jean Santeuil*.

The first impression, as I have just described it, would however soon appear inadequate. An observant reader, when he had perused a chapter or two, would find that subjects which had seemed detached, separate and finished with, actually recur to be further developed and involved with other subjects which receive similar treatment; and gradually a different impression arises. The composition of the work as a whole is seen to be more like that of a symphony and less like the hazards of a diary: the different subjects reappear like themes and *motifs* in musical composition. In other words, the work is a *literary* composition, elaborated with great skill on a basis of autobiography. Although the term has been abused in frivolous connections, Proust's novel is essentially a kind of 'romanced autobiography', in which many of the numerous figures and details become significant and contribute towards an integrated impression, imaginative, philosophic and critical, on a vast scale, of the life of his time. Despite the diversity of its aspects, we come to see that the novel Proust had not completely revised before he died is far more closely knit and integrated than any of those earlier achievements with which it has been compared or contrasted: Zola's study of the *Rougon-Macquart* family, Balzac's *Comédie humaine*, or that other great portrait of a society in decline, Saint-Simon's *Memoirs of the Reign of Louis XIV*.

Now one would assume that the success of an autobiographical effort, begun on the threshold of maturity, must depend very largely on the author's powers of memory and evocation. Proust had a prodigious memory: Maurois speaks of its terrible recreative power. The number of different things recalled is extraordinary. And when we think of the detail in which they are described, even when allowances are made for the art of elaboration and for the imaginative treatment, we perceive that the genius of Proust is inseparable from the intensive power of his superior gift. Of this he showed himself better aware than anyone else when he gave for general title to the first and greater part of his novel the now famous rubric: *A la Recherche du Temps perdu*.

It is a magnificent phrase and very Proustian: it has

amplitude, sonority and depth of implication. First the effort to recover something so precious that a man of great gifts and wealth and position should sacrifice all—as Proust did, with his health and life—to this one task of recovering time lost. But what is meant by time here? Not chronological time surely? It is not a measurement in moments or in centuries that Proust is in quest of; it is *duration*, something that has filled a space of life with experience. Note that the main incidence of Proust's quest, his real effort at recovery is concentrated on that part of experience that is lost to memory—dead even to the resuscitating powers of *his* memory. Note also that this precious pearl of experience is not lost in the 'dark backward and abysm of time' (to use a still more famous phrase). Proust is not writing an historical novel. What is lost has been lost in less than half a lifetime: it has slipped away with youth beyond recall.

Few titles could therefore be more inadequate as a substitute than the one which a justly praised translation has made popular in this country. Proust's title means anything but 'Remembrance of things past'. What his phrase suggests is the *recovery of the irretrievable*. It has an elegiac strain: and what makes it the more poignant is that the irretrievable—as in elegy—has been lost within the space of a life that has survived it.

But now we must remind ourselves that Proust is by no means solely interested in the mysteries and metaphysics of memory: he has a genial grasp of the concrete that reminds one at times of Dickens. The first part of *Du Côté de chez Swann* is called 'Combray', and Combray stands for the home-town of the Proust family—Illiers, near Chartres. But we are not plunged at once into domesticities.

Volume One opens with a long meditation which routed the first publishers whom Proust approached with his manuscript. It is a ruminating analysis of the experiences of sleep, dreams and oblivion, and then of awakening, detachment from the dream and the gradual orientation of the self to the 'real' world of light and shade, room-space and furniture. Little by little, with the help of sensation, the sleeper awakens to consciousness of his place in the home, in the town, in the civilized society of his milieu.

The passage that faces us may test our adaptability to a new style which, when most characteristic, is subtle, sinuous, massive and complex. We soon perceive, however, that it is less difficult than it looks. For Proust is really a clear, fully explicit writer. Difficulties may indeed arise from the complexities of his vision, but he never aims at obscurity. In place of the condensation of Mallarmé's style, which leaves so much out, it is the elaborate complication of Proust's style that can make his prose difficult to unravel; but all the warp and woof is there like the network of threads in shot-silk. In this sense Proust is a classical writer, not a symbolist. Nothing shows this better than the great use he makes of the *simile*, that is the fully balanced comparison with 'as' or 'like'. Note that he uses the simile to complete an exposition, to illustrate a point, to round off a paragraph or to clinch an argument or a meditation. We shall see a good example in a moment; but here we have the simile of a traveller lost in the countryside, looking for a station; and we are told that the traveller will recall later all the details of the route. But only exceptionally observant people could register so many details on their way to catch a train at a distant station which they have first to find! Proust is exceptionally observant of his surroundings, physical, atmospheric, social and especially artistic. He had the most tremulous antennae of all the writers of his time; his sensibility was extreme, maladive. We soon perceive that the person telling the story is a *malade*. It is difficult to avoid the French word: the English 'invalid' being too strong to start with. Proust suffered from asthma; his first severe attack happened when he was nine. As a writer he must be one of the first to make a psychosomatic ailment a major element in a novel. Illness is one of the 'villains of the piece', a tragic element but also a stimulus. One of the results of a malady like Proust's is insomnia, insomnia the 'mother of memory', as Maurois calls it. Thus even his affliction serves our author's ambitious purpose: the recovery of lost time goes on in the wakeful hours of night.

As we have admitted, these early pages may appear discontinuous, but already we notice that some of the themes and persons are beginning to recur. The theme of sleep reappears throughout the first forty pages. The specific reference is to the Narrator's habit of going to bed as a boy without being able to sleep until his mother had come up to wish him 'good night'. This occurred regularly unless there was company: tonight a visit is expected from M. Swann. But before he arrives we meet the family: parents, grandparents, uncles and aunts. They are not presented to us; there are no full-length portraits in the manner of Balzac. We just find them 'at home'.

M. Swann has become a rare visitor, and inspires one of those interminable discussions about social status which fascinates Proust. The great-aunt's view is that people should keep the rank to which they were born or their original station in society. To go up is as bad as to go down. She does not know that Swann has risen in society (as Proust himself will do) to associate with duchesses and princes. The old lady has deceived herself by holding to a view of Swann which is her own but no longer true of Swann as he is. Her foible is treated with a gentle touch of irony; but it leads to one of Proust's favourite contentions. We know people not as they are but as *personae* that we make up and project onto them, without wishing to know them in reality. This new theme emerges but for a moment. We shall see its importance later in the treatment of Swann's love affair. Here we could scarcely detect an ominous note in the observation: 'Même l'acte si simple que nous appelons "voir une personne que nous connaissons" est en partie un acte intellectuel.'

After this digression on Swann's evening call, we return to the scene in the child's bedroom. The crisis is reached when the father who wants to discourage his son's timidity behaves with sudden caprice and bids the mother spend the night in the child's room: she sends him to sleep by reading stories from George Sand. These episodes are treated with great simplicity; they are very human, very real. How many eldest or only sons before Marcel's time and since have played that solemn little prank with their mother's feelings, and how many strict fathers have given way with as much irascible grace as the Narrator's to his son's appeal from the top of the stairs!

A few dots separate the next section which evidently represents an afterthought or a reflexion on the incidents already recorded. Actually this appendix, if I may call it so, is one of the most important passages in the whole of Proust's writings. He reminds us of a Celtic legend about the souls of the dead that remain imprisoned in things and can be liberated only by chance when they are unexpectedly *recognized* by us as we pass: then the soul escapes the captivity of living death.

This little story helps to focus our attention on the mysterious central experience which comes next.

Il y avait déjà bien des années que, de Combray, tout ce qui n'était pas le théâtre et le drame de mon coucher n'existait plus pour moi, quand un jour d'hiver, comme je rentrais à la maison, ma mère, voyant que j'avais froid, me proposa de me faire prendre, contre mon habitude, un peu de thé. Je refusai d'abord et, je ne sais pourquoi, je me ravisai. Elle envoya chercher un de ces gâteaux courts et dodus appelés Petites Madeleines qui semblent avoir été moulés dans la valve rainurée d'une coquille de Saint-Jacques. Et bientôt, machinalement, accablé par la morne journée et la perspective d'un triste lendemain, je portai à mes lèvres une cuillerée du thé où j'avais laissé s'amollir un morceau de madeleine. Mais à l'instant même où la gorgée mêlée des miettes du gâteau toucha mon palais, je tressaillis, attentif à ce qui se passait d'extraordinaire en moi. Un plaisir délicieux m'avait envahi, isolé, sans la notion de sa cause. Il m'avait aussitôt rendu les vicissitudes de la vie indifférentes, ses désastres inoffensifs, sa brièveté illusoire, de la même façon qu'opère l'amour, en me remplissant d'une essence précieuse: ou plutôt cette essence n'était pas en moi, elle était moi. J'avais cessé de me sentir médiocre, contingent, mortel. D'où avait pu me venir cette puissante joie? Je sentais qu'elle était liée au goût du thé et du gâteau, mais qu'elle le dépassait infiniment, ne devait pas être de même nature. D'où venait-elle? Que signifiait-elle? Où l'appréhender?... Arrivera-t-il jusqu'à la surface de ma claire conscience, ce souvenir, l'instant ancien que l'attraction d'un instant identique est venue de si loin solliciter, émouvoir, soulever tout au fond de moi? Je ne sais. Maintenant je ne sens plus rien, il est arrêté, redescendu peut-être; qui sait s'il remontera jamais de sa nuit? Dix fois il me faut recommencer, me pencher vers lui. Et chaque fois la lâcheté qui nous détourne de toute tâche difficile, de toute œuvre importante, m'a conseillé de laisser cela, de boire mon thé en pensant simplement à mes ennuis d'aujourd'hui, à mes désirs de demain qui se laissent remâcher sans peine.

Et tout d'un coup le souvenir m'est apparu. Ce goût, c'était celui du petit morceau de madeleine que le dimanche matin, à Combray (parce que ce jour-là je ne sortais pas avant l'heure de la messe), quand j'allais lui dire bonjour dans sa chambre, ma tante Léonie m'offrait après l'avoir trempé dans son infusion de thé ou de tilleul. La vue de la petite madeleine ne m'avait rien rappelé avant que je n'y eusse goûté; peut-être parce que, en ayant souvent aperçu depuis, sans en manger, sur les tablettes des pâtissiers, leur image avait quitté ces jours de Combray pour se lier à d'autres plus récents; peut-être parce que, de ces souvenirs abandonnés si longtemps hors de la mémoire, rien ne survivait, tout s'était désagrégé; les formes—et celle aussi du petit coquillage de pâtisserie, si grassement sensuel sous son plissage sévère et dévot —s'étaient abolies, ou, ensommeillées, avaient perdu la force d'expansion qui leur eût permis de rejoindre la conscience. Mais, quand d'un passé ancien rien ne subsiste, après la mort des êtres, après la destruction des choses, seules, plus frêles mais plus vivaces, plus immatérielles, plus persistantes, plus fidèles, l'odeur et la saveur restent encore longtemps comme des âmes, à se rappeler, à attendre, à espérer, sur la ruine de tout le reste, à porter sans fléchir, sur leur gouttelette presque impalpable, l'édifice immense du souvenir.

Whatever you have seen in this episode you cannot have missed a characteristic paradox: an experience of mysterious significance for the Narrator has developed from a very commonplace incident. The taste of the *madeleine* dipped in the tea fills him with a strange pleasure. The sensation, which he interrogates again and again, at last of its own accord yields a forgotten memory of Combray, a similar experience he had as a boy when a bed-ridden aunt gave him a morsel soaked in tea or *tilleul* which she was taking for breakfast. What is important here is that a chance *sensation* has stimulated what Proust calls elsewhere an 'involuntary memory'. Suddenly a key to the past seems to have been placed in his hand; but it is a key he cannot use at will. The liberating sensation cannot be deliberately induced; it comes unawares. But when it comes it brings, not only a reminiscence, but a flood of feeling, and the realization that a depth of oblivion has been probed and that something has emerged from the unfathomable.

Note once more that the sensation, which it would be better to call a *clue* than a key, is accompanied by a feeling of elation: Proust says 'of joy'. I hope it will not seem incongruous if I remind you that in a book called *Surprised by Joy*,

Dr C. S. Lewis has analysed varieties of an experience not unlike Proust's, but occurring in a temperament and to a personality very different from his. Most of you will also remember that the phrase, 'Surprised by joy', comes from one of Wordsworth's greatest sonnets,—Wordsworth, the author of the *Ode on the Intimations of Immortality*, which again is concerned with the same mysterious phenomenon of recollection.

Proust brings his meditation to a close with another simple but charming comparison. Gradually, he realizes, the whole past may open out like the little Japanese game composed of bits of paper which expand in water to reveal a subaqueous world of diminutive flowers, trees and homesteads.

It is curiously apposite for us here to recall that the fascination Proust felt for this miniature plaything was one of the many gifts he owed to a friend who has survived him and to whom we too are grateful for the support she has given to this exhibition and to the study of Proust everywhere.[1]

The second part of *Du Côté de Chez Swann* is the famous episode, *Un Amour de Swann*. This is clearly a section which does not fit into the chronology of events as they have appeared in the Narrator's sequence. Indeed it is not at all a part of what we might call the Narrator's novel but a fragment interpolated from a different novel Proust had planned to write on Swann, but threw up in favour of the work we know. Yet as M. Swann is an important figure in Proust's novel, the episode about his love affair cannot be regarded as an *hors-d'œuvre*: it has vital connections with the work in which it is placed. Here we see Proust not as an introspective psychologist but as an analyst of sexual love—one is forced to say a destructive analyst—and as a psychologist of society.

[1] The reference here is to the late Mrs Nordlinger-Riefstahl who presided when this paper was read at an exhibition of Proustian relics held at the Whitworth Gallery, Manchester, in May 1956.

It is known that the young Marcel made his début in Parisian society at the age of fifteen and published his first book, *Les Plaisirs et les Jours*, in 1896. But this episode does not transport us at once into high society: we find ourselves at first involved in the 'petit noyau' or 'petit groupe' or 'petit clan' firmly centred in Mme Verdurin. It is a milieu of middle-class snobs, obviously 'pseudo' but unconventional, lively and amusing. The presentation of the Verdurin group is highly satirical and often very humorous. Mme Verdurin has dislocated her jaw and cannot laugh as violently as usual (that is she cannot *rire aux larmes*). So to play up the spirit of her circle she mimes her own outbursts and holds her jaw in place. She is very well done, generous, possessive, talkative and tiresome, and so are Dr Cottard and the Sorbonnards: like so many intellectuals they are not really intelligent.

It is Cottard who introduces Swann to the Verdurins, and there he finds Odette de Crécy. Swann himself is an endearing figure, genuinely refined and intelligent. He sees through the clichés, the forced hilarity and clannishness of the milieu, but he cannot break away because of Odette. She obsesses him; and the love affair is not so much a study of sexual attraction as a prototype of the thraldom of cerebral obsession which dominates a later part of the novel, when the Narrator's mind will be fixed on Albertine.

You will remember Proust's belief that we do not know people as they are, but project upon them the people we want them to be. *Un Amour de Swann* is a study of the growth of an illusion of this kind and of the suspicions increasing in the mind of the enamoured man that he is deceiving himself. From the first Swann has been drawn to Odette not by her own charms, which are modest, but largely by their resemblance to features in the works of certain great artists, Michelangelo and Botticelli. 'He placed', we read, 'on his study table, *as if* it were a photograph of Odette, a reproduction of the daughter of Jethro.' This is anything but art for art's sake, this case of a man using reproductions of works of art to stimulate his love for a woman. The photograph makes up for the desires he has not been able to feel fully realized in the person of the woman; and the difficult question arises—though not for discussion here—as to whether Proust ever succeeds in depicting hetero-sexual love: the relationship when he attempts to treat it always seems to change into some other relationship or to wither away. True love deteriorates. Odette becomes Madame Swann, the friend of Baron de Charlus; and Albertine disappears . . .

Gradually hints of the truth break through the illusion. The observations of the Verdurins point to the kind of person Odette really is—not without attraction but neither virtuous nor intelligent. And there is a pathetic scene when Swann, feeling Odette's affection for him to be 'un peu courte', attempts to enliven it by making her play the phrase from Vinteuil's sonata of which he is passionately fond. She strums it on an untuned piano while he bends over and kisses her twenty times! So the refinement of Swann's feeling is degraded by a delusion he tries to cherish against his doubts.

Yet a kind of compensation emerges from this dubious relationship. Swann recovers something of the thrill of his original artistic reactions, this time experienced through his interest in another person. The world of art is the real world for Swann as it is for Proust, the only world of the spirit left for modern man to enter. Love is one of its keys and Swann re-enters the world of art through his relationship with Odette and despite the fact that he is already afraid that, as a love affair, it is not going to be much of a success. Actually, as I have indicated, when first we meet Odette it is as Mme Swann in the park of Tansonville: she is the mother of Gilberte, but her companion is not her husband but the notorious Baron de Charlus.

Swann has made Odette his wife after all, despite her lack of intelligence and her defective feeling for the arts. How could this have happened? Here the curve of Proust's searching analysis comes full circle. Love in Proust is not only stimulable through association with the arts; it can be kept alive by suspicion and jealousy. Indeed sexual love can be transformed into jealousy. Of Swann he tells us: 'il avait fait de la jalousie avec son amour'.

The ravages of this obsession are given a final exhibition in a scene more pathetic and humiliating even than the scene at the piano. Returning late one evening from Odette's abode, Swann is seized with suspicion of her relations to another member of the Verdurin group, the Comte de Forcheville, and he makes his way back to the obscure street in which she lives. Only one window is alight. He peers through but cannot detect clearly who is in the room beyond. At last he knocks: strangers come to the door. He appears to have mistaken the house and withdraws in confusion, a confusion that involves the reader. We never quite know whether he had been deceived this time or not. All we know is that his affection for Odette has involved him in a shady world of duplicity and doubt.

We are about to tire of Swann's abortive love affair when the author raises the whole level of the episode and carries us aloft through music into metaphysics again.

Swann has broken with the Verdurins because they omitted to invite him to a house party; he reverts to the higher level among his acquaintances which is really his milieu, and we find him at a soirée given by the Marquise de Sainte-Euverte. There he hears Chopin played and the 'St Francis of Liszt': that must be the fantasia called 'Saint Francis preaching to the birds'. Members of the Proustian aristocracy arrive, Mme de Cambremer and the Princesse de Laumes. After much trivial chatter, Swann rises to leave, when his favourite sonata by Vinteuil is played. The little phrase fills him with anguish because of its association with Odette. But there is more in it than that. . . .

We have already had occasion to notice that Proust becomes preoccupied from time to time not with the events the Narrator is recounting but with the significance of certain 'privileged moments' (as the French call them), moments of insight or of 'shadowy recollection' (to borrow Wordsworth's phrase). Such moments seem unaccountably rich and precious, yet we may not fully recognize their value when first they occur. They are forgotten, buried in the past or lost in the unconscious from which something intrinsically insignificant may recall or release them. Then they return to us enriched and incrusted with deep feeling or strange joy—beyond reality: supernatural; beyond time: eternal; beyond death: immortal. All this may be felt only in the flash of recovery and may be lost again. But it gives to these unchallengeable moments an inexplicable wonder, a touch of the truly marvellous, of vision, of profundity. Now these are the nuclei which, extended and intensified, constitute for Proust the essential experience of the artist. At this point Proust's thought seems to me to touch and expand beyond the aesthetic intuitions of Baudelaire, one or two of whose favourite terms and images we detect embedded in Proust's argument. Both were realists, but each at his highest and deepest moments could touch the peaks and fundaments of Platonic idealism. Distant reverberations of the *Symposium* pass like tremors through the tension of their thought.

Read the remarkable meditation prompted in the mind of Swann as his favourite phrase of music emerges above the talk in Mme de Sainte-Euverte's party:

Mais le concert recommença et Swann comprit qu'il ne pourrait pas s'en aller avant la fin de ce nouveau numéro du programme. Il souffrait de rester enfermé au milieu de ces gens dont la bêtise et les ridicules le frappaient d'autant plus douloureusement qu'ignorant son amour, incapables, s'ils l'avaient connu, de s'y intéresser et de faire autre chose que d'en sourire comme d'un enfantillage ou de le déplorer comme une folie, ils le lui faisaient apparaître sous l'aspect d'un état subjectif qui n'existait que pour lui, dont rien d'extérieur ne lui affirmait la réalité; il souffrait surtout, et au point que même le son des instruments lui donnait envie de crier, de prolonger son exil dans ce lieu où Odette ne viendrait jamais, où personne, où rien ne la connaissait, d'où elle était entièrement absente.

Mais tout à coup ce fut comme si elle était entrée, et cette apparition lui fut une si déchirante souffrance qu'il dut porter la main à son cœur. C'est que le violon était monté à des notes hautes où il restait comme pour une attente, une attente qui se prolongeait sans qu'il cessât de les tenir, dans l'exaltation où il était d'apercevoir déjà l'objet de son attente qui s'approchait, et avec un effort désespéré pour tâcher de durer jusqu'à son arrivée, de l'accueillir avant d'expirer, de lui maintenir encore un moment de toutes ses dernières forces le chemin ouvert pour qu'il pût passer, comme on soutient une porte qui sans cela retomberait. Et avant que Swann eût eu le temps de comprendre, et de se dire: 'C'est la petite phrase de la sonate de Vinteuil, n'écoutons pas!' tous ses souvenirs du temps où Odette était éprise de lui, et qu'il avait réussi jusqu'à ce jour à maintenir invisibles dans les profondeurs de son être, trompés par ce brusque rayon du temps d'amour qu'ils crurent revenu, s'étaient réveillés et, à tire d'aile, étaient remontés lui chanter éperdument, sans pitié pour son infortune présente, les refrains oubliés du bonheur.

Proust is a French writer, and if, as we suggest, the cult of the privileged moment is shared by him with Wordsworth and many other modern writers, we now must ask, has he not a way of his own of experiencing and transmitting this type of mental phenomenon?

One obvious distinction can at least be made in conclusion. Among the central facts of Proust's life and work were certain modes of recollection to which he attached great value. They were experienced by a person endowed with something like the vision of a contemplative combined with social gifts of a superior order, the exercise of which contributed much to his insight as a novelist but at the expense of diverting his attention to the allurements and dissipations of the most fascinating society in the world. That these diversions prevented him from realizing to the full gamut of his sensibility certain moments of exceptional premonition seems clear from the number of occasions we notice him trying to withdraw from company, so as to concentrate on some irruption from the unconscious and search down to its roots. And we know that for the last third of his life, though dying in self-imposed quarantine, he strove to keep his mind in a state of high tension on a diet of drugs and coffee, the better to concentrate on his work.

From the heavily curtained bed in the corklined room, with its sealed windows and subdued light, the extraordinary eyes look out of the emaciated visage, but not listlessly into empty space. Like powerful searchlights they turn on one aspect after another of the bygone panorama. But now, sensibility, imagination and analysis are at grips with it, unencumbered as they were never before. The past is experienced in its purity, decontaminated of contacts with ordinary experience and cleansed of the dross of the contingent. Preserved intact by memory the treasure of time that was lost is recovered in a rapture of absolute possession and held in the moment of pure contemplation which leads to the highest illuminations of art. So in his unforgettable impression of Venice, the lamps of the gondolas seem to conduct the dark waters of the canal back to the heart of the city of his dreams.

XII

ANDRÉ GIDE
ANGLES OF APPROACH

We are all familiar with C. G. Jung's division of human beings into two basic types: extrovert and introvert. I do not remember having seen a psycho-analysis of André Gide; but I assume he should be placed in the introverted category. This, however, is a categorical placing of the man and his work which is not the one I want to begin with. I find it more useful to introduce Gide by contrasting mental types in a different way, namely into the unified and the diversified.

In the unified type the mind is devoted to, or tends to be obsessed by, one great idea which dominates the complexities of the man's nature and constrains him to concentrate his energies on some chosen task or single interest. It is the mind of the leader of men or the founder of a cause. St Paul would be a good example of the man of one idea with no shadow of turning. I suggest too that the characteristics of the unified mind are found in the supreme creative type whether in the arts or the sciences, in religion or in empire-building. Gide is decidedly not of this type.

The other type, the diversified mind, never rises above its complexities. It remains contradictory within itself and works successively and even simultaneously in opposite directions. 'Ambivalent' and 'bi-polar' are epithets applied to its powers since such a mind can swing from one extreme to another and appreciate both. It is, as Sainte-Beuve suggested in a well-known passage on Bayle, the opposite of the 'one-way' mind, always on guard against prejudice. The title of one of Gide's lesser works is *Un esprit non prévenu* (1929). That is what he strove to be: an unprejudiced mind. And that he did not succeed only proves he was human.

The diversified mind is essentially the critical type, skilled in understanding disparities; curious about the differences between men in themselves, in their social situations, in their racial distinctions. Such mentalities tend to be tolerant and sympathetic through the habit of balancing diversities and looking at both sides—or if possible at all sides—of the case. The best examples of such minds are not constructive, but they can appreciate and evaluate the forces, impulses and motives behind constructive effort, and they can face the fact that some of the strongest and deepest springs of action are destructive. In this way they approach the fundamental problem of good and evil: what promotes the good life and what corrupts it. Such mentalities have been called 'experiencing minds'. Montaigne is, I suppose, the supreme example in France; André Gide is a conspicuous modern example.

The type to which Gide conforms is uninventive and unimaginative in the great creative sense. Gide confessed his inability to write a novel: at least he avoided giving the name to any he had written before *Les Faux-Monnayeurs* of 1926; and even this work is largely autobiographical. His characters tend to reflect aspects of his personality and problems. This is not an uncommon trait among novelists, many of whom write a first draft and repeat the type by varying the theme and characterization in their later productions. What is marked in Gide's 'novels', which he began by calling *récits* (tales) or *soties* (satirical farces), is the elaborate use he makes of diaries, intimate journals, journals about novel writing, about writing *this* novel—all of which conform in substance to the main series of his personal *Journaux*, begun in 1889 and terminated in 1939. These constitute his major work—the work of a great modern introspective—a self watching his every movement, impulse, variation; interrogating his motives, annotating his thoughts almost before they have crystallized into concepts.

The journals face us with this paradox. On the one hand Gide, a monster of instability, perpetually pursuing the variations of his own personality, yet without being able to track down the self. In his last jottings, a few days before he died he wrote: 'I don't hit it off, I have never been able to hit it off completely with reality. Properly speaking, it is not even a result of dissociation that someone, in me, is always observer of the one who acts. No, it is the very one who acts, or who suffers, who doesn't take himself seriously. I even believe that at the moment of death I shall say to myself: "Look! He's dying." '[1]

Yet the very instability of the man, the ambivalence of his tendencies, the pendulum swing from one extreme to the other, make it impossible for us to describe him as a personality dissolving in self-analysis. While we were doing that he would escape and pass over from a negative to a positive position. And the personality that we thought was going to disintegrate in its own analytical crucible, crystallizes into the champion of the liberty of the individual, whether black or white, against the powers of the state, of finance, or superstition—the man who feels compassion for the suffering, the enslaved, the exploited, and who can write a book on the Congo which provides the Chambre des Députés with a document on the strength of which the Minister promises that the big rubber concessions will not be renewed.

But of course Proteus cannot remain positive for long. The anti-colonist, the anti-capitalist becomes an enthusiast

[1] *So be it* (trans. of *Ainsi soit-il*), p. 133.

for Communism in the 30's, and accepts an invitation to Russia. There he travels widely, is entertained and fêted. He is shown not everything, but a little too much. One day finding himself in Stalin's native place on an anniversary of the dictator's birth, he seizes the opportunity to send him congratulations by wire. The interpreters jib at the bare word 'vous' and insist on adding a flattering phrase. Gide protests but has to yield, lamenting the distance that such compliments fix between the 'chef des travailleurs' and the people. Back swings the pendulum from enthusiasm to caution. Gide writes his *Retour de l'URSS* (1936), and follows it up with *Retouches* (1937), against what he now calls 'L'Eglise nouvelle, les nouveaux dogmes, la nouvelle théocratie'.

These changes of direction, these oscillations of sympathy and revulsion exasperated the Russians; they may irritate us too. Gide has a way of arriving at some illuminating conclusion which, no sooner reached and proclaimed than back he goes upon his tracks until you begin to distrust what he gives you as truth, and to conclude that all with him is feeling, the feeling of the moment and the mood, as it was so often with Rousseau. But Gide knows how to justify his vagaries. To Paul Souday he confessed: 'Je suis un être de dialogue et non point d'affirmation.' The complexities of his own psychology he appraises in this characteristic phrase: 'Ma valeur est dans ma complication.' His oscillations make him 'toujours disponible'. And note that ultimately Gide evades judgement on his shifts and contradictions by claiming that he was essentially an artist—the artist who knows how to present the problem, how to dramatize the conflict, but who does not offer to solve problems or to end conflicts by contriving the victory of one side over the other.

Can we offer any explanation of this extraordinary changeableness of temperament, this unstable fluctuation between extremes each of which seems thoroughly realized and understood only to be abandoned? Let us glance at Gide's origins.

Born in Paris in 1869, he described himself as 'the product of two races, two provinces, two faiths (or confessions)'; and again, as the son of a father from Uzès and a mother from Normandy. The boy's father died when he was eleven, leaving his only child an heir to much wealth.

The Gides, originally of peasant stock, were Calvinists of the Cévennes. The family rose in wealth and status to the level of Huguenot *grands bourgeois*. This decidedly intelligent stock had, in the generation before André's birth, produced an eminent economist in Charles Gide, joint author of a once famous textbook familiarly known as 'Gide et Rist'.

The boy was brought up by three elderly, intelligent but rather staid ladies: his mother, his Aunt Claire and Miss Anna Shackleton, who had been the Scots governess of Gide's mother. Madame Gide, who came of a good Rouen family, was devoted to her son, but as Henri Clouard puts it, 'elle le gâtait avec sévérité'. The boy's childhood passed in a puritanical *ambiance* that was probably not harsh but which definitely set its mark upon him. It is most likely that the gravity of his upbringing helped to produce what we call a 'problem child', and that Gide's ultimate resentment against family life and, more generally, against asceticism and prohibitions, had its roots in the relation of the boy to his mother and to his early Calvinist milieu. The grown man found this influence stifling. His reaction is expressed through the words of Armand in *Les Faux-Monnayeurs*, when he speaks of 'la haine de tout ce qu'on appelle vertu', which is engendered by a puritan education. And M. Clouard reminds us that in the Protestant tradition, 'virtue' means 'restrictions'.

On the positive side, the way Gide was brought up helped

to direct his attention to some of the most serious of human problems. As he says in the Notes scribbled shortly before his death: 'My heredity and then my Protestant upbringing turned my mind almost exclusively towards moral problems.'[1]

Here comes another paradox. Many of Gide's works could hardly be recommended to the young as studies in strict morality. Early in this century some of them came under severe criticism in France as the productions of a subversive, even of a corrupting, thinker. Such is not likely to be the considered verdict of posterity. When his first, Symbolist phase was over, Gide's mind and work became absorbed in human, ethical and social problems which he envisaged, presented and debated from endlessly different angles and opposed standpoints. Our judgement must be directed to the whole of his work, not to parts. We must gauge his merits on the balance between his extremes and forbear to assess them on one extreme position rather than on another.

We have characterized Gide's home circumstances as typical of the French Protestant bourgeoisie, puritan in judgement and strict in behaviour; but we must not forget to add, exceptionally civilized. Madame Gide saw that her son received a good musical and artistic education; her companion, Miss Shackleton, translated from the classics and botanized, and the boy gained a life's interest in these studies, becoming soon an expert amateur pianist on his way to being an enormous reader and a rare literary critic.

It seems hardly too much to say that Gide's youth and early manhood were illuminated by his association with the woman he called 'Emmanuèle'. She was Madeleine Rondeaux, his cousin on the maternal side, and who shared and stimulated the idealistic and platonic aspirations of his nature.

[1] *So be it*, p. 31.

They read Greek and the Bible together, as well as Shakespeare, Pascal and Bossuet, 'intoxicated', it has been said, 'with a common spiritual ardour'. The biblical myths and parables provided—to an unusual degree with a modern French writer—the themes of some of Gide's mature works, and the cadences of Scripture are audible in his rhythms. This is evident in what is the most beautiful of all his writings —his version of the parable of the Prodigal Son. In *La Symphonie pastorale* reminiscences of biblical themes and rhythms again appear, though now they tend to be treated ironically. The author of this work has advanced a long way from the positions of his fervent adolescence—or has he retrogressed?

Gide himself summed up the main influences of this period of initiation in the following phrase, which I translate: 'Without this Christian education (*formation*), without these links and bonds, without Emmanuèle who guided my pious inclinations, I should not have written *André Walter* or *L'Immoraliste* or *La Porte étroite* or *La Symphonie pastorale* or *Les Caves du Vatican*, or even perhaps *Les Faux-Monnayeurs* as a protest and reaction.' 'Certainly,' says a commentator, 'in Gide's portrayal of women, his wife is ubiquitously present: they bear the stamp of his marriage and its extraordinary character.'

Anyone ignorant of the Gidean background might ask at this point, where is the evidence of the contrast between the two faiths or confessions of which he speaks? Some critics query the suggestion.

André's paternal ancestry had been Protestant since the Reformation. On his mother's side the line was Catholic until 1839, thirty years before André's birth, when his grandfather became Protestant, married a lady of the same persuasion and consented to have his children brought up in that religion. And although one of his sons returned to the

Roman faith, Gide's mother remained a firm Protestant. Yet her son seems to have been unable to forget the Catholic strain he inherited through her.

In 1895 André married his first cousin, Madeleine Rondeaux. Doubting whether such a union would be happy, his uncle, Charles Gide, wrote to the young man's mother with scholarly caution: 'Yet if it does not take place, both of them will almost surely be unhappy; so there remains only a choice between a *certain* evil and a probable one.' Gide himself wrote later in his Journal: 'Fate was leading me on, also perhaps a secret need to challenge my nature: for was it not virtue itself that I loved in her? It was heaven that my insatiable hell was marrying.'

The marriage was a tragedy, the developing horror of which is painfully exaggerated in one of Gide's masterpieces, the novel called *L'Immoraliste*. This appeared in 1902. With *La Porte étroite* of 1909, the pendulum has swung from the extreme of self-centred indulgence and wilful aberration to the excess of piety. The autobiographical element in the new novel is large. The spiritual relationship between the two cousins, Alissa and Jérôme, reflects that of Madeleine and André. The death of Jérôme's father when the boy is eleven, the sketch of his widowed mother, and the further portrait of Miss Ashburton, faithfully reproduce the details of Gide's life. The adultery and eventual flight of Alissa's mother correspond to the facts revealed about Madeleine's mother. The pages devoted to the estate in the novel describe that of Cuverville, where Madeleine grew up and André spent most of his vacations.

These details I take from Professor Justin O'Brien.[1] M. Jean Delay confirms them in his fuller account of Gide's

---

[1] To his *Portrait of André Gide* this chapter is indebted for several facts and a few judgements. The quotations come from pp. 215, 218 and 222, with the kind permission of Messrs Secker and Warburg.

early life. If I may obtrude a judgement, *La Porte étroite* is, I think, after Gide's rendering of the Prodigal Son, the most beautiful work he has left us. Of Alissa's journal he expressed the belief that it was the best thing he had written. And he repeatedly insisted that *La Porte étroite* and *L'Immoraliste* were pendants one to the other, the two subjects having developed together in their author's mind, 'the excess of the one finding a secret permission in the excess of the other and the two together establishing a balance'. An observation of Professor O'Brien's is worth quoting here: 'No matter', he says, 'how sympathetically and eloquently Gide presents Alissa's intense mysticism, he also makes clear how empty and useless it is. Besides thwarting Jérome without his complete consent, it even fails to bring her satisfaction and she dies miserably alone, abandoned even of God.'

Alissa's is the tragedy of excessive scruple. The tragedy in *La Symphonie pastorale* is that of excessive self-deception. And if any of your pupils[1] react to the book in the way some students of mine used to do, you may have the task of persuading them that it is not a case of conscious effort to deceive. One strong-minded student, I remember, would have it that the Minister in the story was a deliberate hypocrite. This interpretation, I think you will agree, would make the story far simpler and less subtle than Gide intended it to be; but it might raise the question whether for some readers his portrayal of the unconscious hypocrite has not been pushed too far, that is, whether a man playing the role of the Pastor in the story could carry it through without ever realizing that his motives were impure?

With the help of a few more hints from the author and his commentators let us look a little further into the writing of this tale. In later life Gide admitted: 'I would not swear that

[1] Addressed to teachers of French at a seminar held by Professor R. C. Knight at University College, Swansea, November 1962.

at a certain period of my life I was not very close to being converted.' Then he adds: 'Thank God, however, a few converts among my friends took care of that.' A polite way of saying that their importunities may have obstructed his spiritual progress.

The period of tentative enlightenment to which Gide refers corresponds to that of the First World War, during which he put together some penetrating notes on spiritual themes. These meditations he collected and published at first in a private limited edition in the year 1922. Then, to the scandal of his friends, he republished them in a popular edition four years later to appear at the same time as his autobiographical sketch, *Si le grain ne meurt*, with its 'shocking' personal revelations. This could hardly be called a harmful book. But, with some justification it might be considered a stroke of bad taste on Gide's part to have brought out the two works in rapid succession.

Written during the year 1918 *La Symphonie pastorale* reflects critically on the very type of mysticism its author was simultaneously expressing in the notebook ultimately called *Numquid et tu?* 'Thanks to his strict Calvinist background,' says Justin O'Brien, 'Gide was most familiar with the moral climate that he evokes here. And all his life he had a passion for teaching—like the Pastor who admits in an unguarded moment that he had promised himself great pleasure from educating his blind charge. Furthermore Gide had spent the winter of 1894 in the icy Jura Mountains at inhospitable La Brévine, the scene he chose for his narrative.'

Gide called his novel an exposure of 'a form of lying to oneself', and, again, a criticism of the danger of 'the free interpretation of the Scriptures'. But his most revealing comment is found in a note on the Pastor inserted in a letter he wrote to an American scholar: 'Through him, rather than trying to express my own thoughts, I have depicted the pit-fall to which my own doctrine might lead, when that ethic is not rigorously checked by a critical spirit constantly on the alert and little inclined to self-indulgence. This indispensable critical spirit is completely lacking in the Pastor.'

Gide's mature thought seems to be in continuous reaction against the puritanism of his childhood and youth. Most of his adult life, judged from this early standpoint, was spent in adventures in revolt and experiments in sin, supported by an infinitely elaborate apology which is partly sophistry. Gide cannot get away from the sense of evil. 'The lure of evil', said a Catholic critic, 'much more than the attraction of truth, forms the magnetic centre of the whole of (his) work.'[1]

'Baudelaire', in Mr Eliot's phrase, 'was concerned with Sin and Redemption.' Gide, I should say, was concerned with sin and self-justification. And this involves him in the sophisticated attitudes and arguments that characterize his journals and novels. In all his bigger works he objectifies and externalizes this conflict; but it is always his own. Although with time he loses the sense of God, he cannot escape the example of Christ, and it is not inappropriate that someone should have thought of writing a book called 'Gide and the Hound of Heaven'.

Actually he seems doomed to move between the two poles of the acceptance of Christ and that of the Devil, in whom he claims at times to believe, and who appears to stand for the Eternal Tempter having the whole range of the non-theological virtues at his disposal, offering all the appetites and adventures, indulgences and egoisms of life, as well as the pleasures and satisfactions (many of them legitimate) that the gratification of the instinctive impulses brings with them. The Devil for Gide is not the Anti-Christ but the Anti-Puritan.

That Gide was a courageous thinker must be allowed. He

[1] Le Père Victor Poucel, *L'Esprit d'André Gide*.

lived, as he claimed, a life in which joy was resurgent. He is as far from being a sceptic as from being a believer. Whatever harm it is contended some of his books have done, they were undeniably successful in stimulating curiosity and scrutiny, in sparking off new departures and creative initiatives. They have given to thousands of readers a sense of liberation and freedom from restraint through the dominant interest they show in the problems of adolescence and their evident concern with and for the welfare of the younger generation.

Youth, someone has said, is the matrix of truth for Gide. He demands, in the preface he wrote for *Les Nourritures terrestres* (1897), 'to be placed beside those who have remained true to a youthful ideal'. His interest is sustained by the fact that his psychology is centred, a large part of the time, in sex —'cette curiosité sensuelle', which he admits and which he directs on to all the problems involved, normal and abnormal, ethical and social.

There are no grounds for doubting that Gide wished people to live broader and fuller lives, even at the expense of strict morality and of narrow conceptions of the good life or of obedience to authority supernatural or legal. Gide, one might suggest, was an Adam, uncomfortable in Eden, happier outside, but never quite free from the thought of the Divine Lawgiver, if not of the Avenger. He is always trying to find and to formulate laws of his own to justify his backslidings or to control his eleutheromania. For after all— this is his most fruitful self-contradiction—Gide believes in constraint. His style is there to prove it. And no modern has written so effectively on its value in art: 'L'art naît de contrainte, vit de lutte, meurt de liberté.'

The best summing up of Gide's case that I have come across is the following. It is somewhat condensed, but I'll comment on it in my concluding words: 'His supreme sophistry is his conversion from Christianity to Christ, from law to love which condones every wilful action and every impulse, shedding the fetters of an artificial morality to embrace an ethic of freedom and joy, permitting him full development as a man and an artist.'

The Pastor in *La Symphonie pastorale* is an ironic caricature of the author's tendency to interpret Christ's teaching too freely as a gospel of love without restraints and reservations. But the Gospels record the most severe restrictions. Not long ago a lady who is a poet wrote an article in a joint Oxford and Cambridge review in which she revealed and illustrated so many condemnatory statements in Christ's teaching that she had had to reject it. A bishop, replying, said she ought to read more theology. He did not say which theologians would calm her anxieties. Whether or not the lady was justified in the interpretation she put upon the severest sayings of Christ, Gide himself shows no cognizance of them and seems at times to assume that Christ approved of love in whatever sense, form or fashion. Moreover Gide will have none of the Apostle Paul, who is the lawgiver of the New Testament and for some thinkers the founder of the Church.

But we must not try to be more acute than Gide; he realized the dangers of his own assumptions and he exposes them *consciously* through his unconscious hypocrite, the Pastor.

To end here might leave us in confusion—a confusion contrived by a supremely diversified mind—were it not for one last corrective which he supplied. Gide invited us to judge him finally as an artist. To do so seems to provide the only standpoint from which we can see his variegated and contradictory works fall into a recognizable order. Is it not remarkable that a person so protean in his changes can yet be master of one of the finest styles in twentieth-century prose—a style that appears free from all the excesses and clashes of his thought?

This last glance at Gide, the artist, may suggest the only answer we can give to the vexed question of his sincerity. To indicate its nature I will raise another question which for reasons of space I shall have to leave unsettled. Can a man be sincere if he is notoriously unstable? Does not sincerity imply *consistency* in the personality? Can a protean nature be sincere for long? And if not for long what is meant by a chameleon sincerity? The word seems to lose meaning. Yet men and women of very changeable temperaments are often fine artists. May not the artist be a gifted person who is capable of an intense but intermittent sincerity?

Gide's sincerity is, I think, of this type. It is like the revolving beam of a lighthouse dominating strange coasts and dark seas. It does not bathe them in steady light like the sun's. But when its beam flashes intermittently into their depth, their stark configurations stand out sharply against the circumambient darkness and are seen all the more clearly for the contrast. Man knows himself the better for these penetrating—if partial—scrutinies; and we can safely leave Gide with the last words spoken by his character Thésée: 'Pour le bien de l'humanité future, j'ai fait mon œuvre.'

APPENDIX

A Review of *L'Aventure intellectuelle du XXe siècle. Panorama des littératures européennes* (Nouvelle édition), R.-M. Albérès (Paris, 1959).[1]

It is a serious task to attempt a short notice of a book of such dimensions as this, and the present reviewer could wish it had come into hands more generally competent than his own. The author himself characterizes his work in imposing but not pretentious terms as 'une biographie romancée de la conscience européenne du XXe siècle, vue à travers les principales littératures occidentales'. The first edition appeared ten years ago. In the interval it has been translated into many languages and is still (it is claimed) the only work in France or abroad that gives an account of the evolution of literary sensibility and ideas in Europe since 1900. In other words it aims at being a critical *summa* of the thought of our century, apprehended in its most popular forms of literary expression: the novel, drama, and essay. The poetry of the period makes less demand on the author's space. His book is full of clear, masterly *résumés*, enriched with illuminating *aperçus* and judicious reflections. It is well made and faultlessly produced. The abundant material is arranged in four parts corresponding roughly to successive phases of development. To these is appended a useful set of synoptic tables, subdivided into categories of outstanding examples that extend from the *Brothers Karamazov* (which exceeds the backward limit of reference by twenty years) to productions of the generation of Mr John Wain and Mr Colin Wilson ('enfant prodige de l'essai').

Thanks to his habit of evaluating, M. Albérès's work goes far beyond the descriptive catalogue of types and genres with which

[1] From *French Studies*, Vol. XV with the Editors' permission.

the academic classification of literature is too often content. With one reservation to be mentioned later, more of the kind of treatment he applies would, I think, be beneficial to undergraduate studies. His book should certainly be made available for students of comparative literature. It would show them that the application of comparative method should not stop at detached observations on similarities or differences of form and content, regarded simply as elements of structure or proofs of derivation.

M. Albérès judges. What impression does he give of the nature and value of his multiform material? How do the novelists, playwrights and essayists he is concerned with react to the vital problems of their time?

The intellectual adventure of the last half-century is found to be feverishly diversified but invariably ineffectual. The *enquête* reveals the failure of modern rationalism to satisfy the twentieth-century mind; but it also exposes the various forms of revolt from intellectualism as rapidly superseding one another, without arriving at any positive basis of truth, faith or serenity. Periodically the effort subsides into scepticism or nihilism. But the residual fact is a split of the intelligence, a division between intellect and reality, between truth and instinct, of which the historical pretext was the opposition between Reason and Faith (1880-1920). This opposition M. Albérès relegates to the past, along with the conflict between science and the humanities. The fundamental split of the last half-century has set off a series of revulsions in favour of spontaneity, sincerity, surrealism and irrational fantasy. The 'great adventure' has been this break away. But the attitude of revolt has become endemic, habitual, fashionable, even banal: 'Tu n'es pas heureux? Personne n'est heureux. Ce n'est pas la mode' (quoted on p. 307).

The ultimate diagnosis of this literature of revolt for revolt's sake is an aggressive *nervosité* (p. 375). It is here that the reservation referred to above seems to apply. Actually it was applied by the author himself in his brief Introduction: 'Bien qu'on la croie aujourd'hui peu utile dans l'enseignement, la littérature reste le seul "baromètre" qui permette de prévenir l'avenir et de comprendre le présent.' This confronts us with a dilemma. Does the literature of this half-century, and especially the novel offer good material to choose from in making our selections of modern 'classics'? And if we ignore it, what other barometer have our students to help them to anticipate the future and understand the present?

INDEX

The titles of works whose authorship is indicated in the context are not included.

Adam, Antoine, 147, 148, 149, 151, 153 and n.
Adrian, Lord, 66
Africa, 159
Albérès, R.-M., 99, 190-2
Albertine, 171
Alcan, 44
Aldington, Richard, 107
Alissa, 183, 184, 188
America, 11, 17, 22
Anacreon, 109
Andromache, 127 and n., 128, 130
Anjou, 100
Arland, Marcel, xiv
Armand, 180
Armytage, W. H. G., 62
Arnauld, Antoine, 105
Ashburton, Flora, 183
Asia Minor, 136
Association of Headmasters, Lancashire and Cheshire Branch, x n.
Association of Heads of French Departments, 60n.
Atlantic, 137
Aucassin et Nicolette, 15
Augusta, Empress, 133
Austin, L. J., 129n.
Ayrton, Michael, 148

Babel, 83
Bailey, J. C., 117
Baldensperger, Fernand, 28, 41, 42, 45
Balzac, Honoré de, 162, 165
Bangor, xvii, 90
Banville, Théodore de, 136

Baudelaire, 32, 67, 101, 103, 121-32, 144, 145, 159, 160
Bayet, Albert, 54n.
Bayle, Pierre, 72, 177
Bédier, Joseph, xiv
Beethoven, 124, 129-30
Beeton, Mrs, 51
Belgium, 149, 156
Bembo, 113, 116
Benda, Julien, 72
Berlin, 133
Bernard, Tristan, 25
Bézard, Julien, 43
Bible, The, 106, 182
Board of Education, 79
Boase, A. M., 152-3
Boileau, 42n., 105
Borel, Eugène, 44n.
Bossuet, 42n., 182
Botticelli, 170
Boucher, François, 147
Bourgeois Gentilhomme, Le, 24
Bourgin, H., 54n.
Brentano's, 41n.
Brereton, Geoffrey, 25 and n.
Breton, André, 71
British Association, The, 66
Brothers Karamazov, 190
Brunetière, Ferdinand, 24, 28, 33, 47
Brussels, 40 and n., 41n., 46 and n., 47n., 48n., 49n., 51n., 55n.

Cahen, Albert, 43n.
Callot, 153
Cambremer, Mme de, 172
Cambridge, 69, 188

193

INDEX

Campistron, Jean Galbert de, 50
Cardigan Bay, 19
Cassandre, 112, 113, 116, 119
Catullus, 109
Cellini, Benevenuto, 119
Cévennes, 180
Chambord, 108
Chambre des Députés, 178
Champion, Pierre, 119
Chanson de Roland, La, 5. *See also* Roland
Charlemagne, 25
Charleville, 149
Charlus, Baron de, 171
Chartres, 18
Chateaubriand, 51
Chénier, André, 119
Chevrillon, André, 17
Chopin, 172
Cicero, 17
City of Dreadful Night, 122
Claire (Mme Guillaume Démarest), 180
Claudel, 103
Clouard, Henri, 180
Coleridge, 38
Combray, 163, 166, 167, 168
Common European Community, The, x
Congo, 178
Corbière, Tristan, 134
Corneille, Pierre, 31, 37, 42n., 50
Corneille, Thomas, 50
Cottard, Dr, 170
Cranston, Maurice, 64
Criterion, The, 105

Dark Lady, The, 119
Darmesteter, Arsène, 19
Degas, Edgar, 32, 100
Delay, Jean, 183
Descartes, 72, 91
Desportes, 118
Dickens, Charles, 163
Discours de la Méthode, 92
Disraeli, 4
Don Quixote, 74, 137
Dreyfus Affair, 42
Du Bellay, Joachim, 25, 107

École Normale Supérieure, 34, 37
Eliot, T. S., 84n., 138, 141-4, 186
Emmanuèle, 181. *See also* Rondeaux
Entwistle, W. J., 77n.
Etiemble, xv
Euclid, 95

Faber, Sir Geoffrey, 11n.
Faguet, Emile, 24, 25, 28, 118n.
Farnell, Lewis, 11
Fleurville, Mauté de, 148
Flexner, Abraham, 75
Florence, 52
Focillon, Henri, 51
Fragonard, Nicolas, 147
France, Anatole, 149
Franchet, Henri, 110n., 115
Francis I, 110
François-Poncet, André, 90n.
Fraser, G. S., 90
French Studies, 190n.

Gare de Lyon, 52
Gautier, Léon, 5
Gautier, Théophile, 119
General Education in a Free Society (Harvard Report), 80
George, F. W. A., 73
Germany, 22, 83n.
Gide, André, 176-89
Gide, Mme, 181. *See also* Rondeaux
Gilberte, 171
Gladstone, 4
Glover, T. G., 17 and n.1, 69-70, 71
Goncourt, Edmond et Jules, 147, 148
Gospels, The, 188
Gourmont, Remy de, 33
Goya, 153
Gradgrind, 57
Greek Anthology, 109
Grimm (Grimm's law), 17
Guérard, Albert, 17, 18

Hackett, C. A., 154, 155n., 156
Hamlet, 134
Harlequin, 149
Harvard, 80
Hatzfeld, Adolphe, 19
Hazard, Paul, xiv, 28

INDEX

Henry III, 110
Henry IV, 110
Hogben, Lancelot, 8
Homer, 17
Homme révolté, L', 100
Horace, 119
Hugo, Victor, 18, 31, 32, 117, 124, 137, 152
Hutchins, Robert Maynard, 11

Illiers, 163
Information littéraire, L', 95
Iphigénie, 37
Ivain, 15

Jammes, Francis, 71
Jérome, 183
Jethro, 171
Jourdain, 73
Jowett, Benjamin, 11n.
Jung, C. G., 176
Jura Mountains, 185
Jusserand, J. J., 106

Kenner, Hugh, 142, 143 and n.
Knight, R. C., 73, 184n.

La Chaussée, Nivelle de, 42n.
Laforgue, Jules, 133–45
Lamarck, 41
Lamartine, 67, 132
Lancret, Nicolas, 147
Langlois, Ernest, 45
Lanson, Gustave, xiv, xv, 23–5, 27–59, 89–100
Lapérouse, 33
La Possonnière, 108
La Roche, 149
Larroumet, Gustave, 33, 34, 36, 37, 38
Laumes, Princesse de, 172
Laumonier, Paul, 109, 113, 118n.
Leconte de Lisle, 119, 158
Lee, Leah, 133
Leguay, Pierre, 27
Lemaire de Belges, Jean, 109
Lewis, C. S., 169
Liège, xvi n., xvii.
Listener, The, 64n., 148

Liszt, Franz, ('St Francis of'), 129–130, 172
Longnon, Henri, 114
Louis XIV, 162
Louvre, 122, 127, 128
Love Song of J. Alfred Prufrock, The, 136, 138
Lucifer, 159

Malade Imaginaire, Le, 74
Malherbe, 105
Mallarmé, 32, 67, 100, 101, 102, 132, 151, 153, 164
Manchester, 3n., 169n.
Marais, 37
Marivaux, 33, 71
Marot, Clément, 109, 116
Marullus (Marullo), 109
Maurois, André, 161, 162, 165
Mecca, 150
Mélanges Lanson, 54n.
Memorandum on the Teaching of Modern Languages, 78
Mendès-France, Pierre, 76
Méthode dans les Sciences, La, 44n.
Metz, 146
Michelangelo, 170
Milly, 67
Moberly, Walter, 69
Modern Language Association, 89 and n.1.
Modern Languages (H.M.S.O.), 21n., 60
Modern Languages (periodical), 89n.
Modern Studies (H.M.S.O.), 13n., 85
Monet, Claude, 153
Monod, Gabriel, 45
Mons, 149
Montaigne, xvi, 25, 35, 72, 96, 177
Montevideo, 133
Moore, W. G., 37n., 44n.
Moreau, Pierre, 93
Mornet, Daniel, 27, 36, 50
Muret, Marc-Antoine, 113, 115, 116
Murry, J. Middleton, 113
Musée Pédagogique, 43, 47, 55
Musset, Alfred de, 39

INDEX

Nadal, Octave, 154
Napier, A. S., 13, 20
Napoleon III, 4
National Union of Students, 15
Newman, John Henry, 63
New Statesman and Nation, The, 84n.
New Testament, The, 188
Nolhac, Pierre de, 114, 115, 116, 117n.
Nordlinger-Riefstahl, Marie, 169n.
Normandy, 180
Norwood Report, The, 80
Nyrop, Kr., 16

O'Brien, Justin, 183 and n., 184, 185
Odette de Crécy, 170, 171, 172, 174
Oliver, 25
Ortega y Gasset, 76
Ovid, 128
Oxford, 13, 188
Oxford University Handbook, 11n.

Pactolus, 136
Palmer, H. E., 79
Paneth, Eva, xii n.
Paris, Gaston, 16
Parsifal, 145
Pascal, Blaise, 96, 182
Pater, Walter, 107, 108, 109, 110
Paul, Saint, 189
Peacock, Ronald, 77n.
Péguy, Charles, 37-8
Petrarch, 112, 113, 114, 116
Pierrot, 147
Pindar, 109
Plato, 117
Pléiade, 107, 118
Poe, Edgar Allan, 153
Poucel, le Père Victor, 186n.
Pound, Ezra, 143, 144
Pradon, Jacques, 50
Prévost, Jean, 132
Proteus, 178
Proust, Marcel, 93, 122, 126 and n., 130, 131, 132, 161-75
Psalms, 103
Psaumes (Marot's), 109
Pyrenees, 133

Quennell, Peter, 121
Quinault, Philippe, 50

Rabelais, 25, 28, 71
Racine, 14, 50, 71
Read, Sir Herbert, 38
Rees, Garnet, 158n.
Rembrandt, 51, 124
Renan, 30, 32
Revue de Belgique, 41n.
Revue de l'Histoire, 36n.
Revue de l'Université de Bruxelles, 40n.
Revue du Mois, 44, n.1.
Rhône, 52
Richard, Jean-Pierre, 160
Rimbaud, 102, 103, 137 and n. 140-168
Roland, 5, 25, 67
Rondeaux, Madeleine (Mme André Gide), 181, 183
Ronsard, 25, 105-20
Rousseau, Jean-Jacques, 179
Roustan, Mario, 94, 95
Royal Society, The, 65
Rubens, 51, 148
Rudler, Gustave, 43, 45, 47, 55, 56, 57
Russell, Bertrand, 6
Russia, 179. See also URSS

Saint-Arnaud, Chevalier de, 4
Sainte-Beuve, 39, 40, 41, and n.2, 42, 109, 176
Sainte-Euverte, Marquise de, 172, 173
Saint-Gelais, Mellin de, 109
Saint-Simon, 162
Sancho Panza, 74
Sand, George, 166
Scapin, 147
Scaramouche, 147
Schneider, René, 51
Seignobos, Charles, 45
Shackleton, Anna, 180, 181
Shakespeare, 118, 119, 124, 158, 182
Sheffield, 62
Shelley, 158
Simon, Pierre-Henri, 23n.

INDEX

Sivry, Charles de, 148
Sorbonne, 51
Souday, Paul, 179
Spitzer, Leo, xvi
Sprat, Thomas, 65
Stalin, 179
Starnbergersee, 132
Stebbing, Susan, 65
Strasbourg, Oaths of, 71
Studies in Modern French Literature, 3n., 158n.
Swann, 161–74
Swansea, 184
Swinburne, 132
Symons, Arthur, 154

Taine, Hippolyte, xv, 32, 33, 39, 40, 41, 55, 68
Tarbes, 133
Tannhäuser, 145
Tansonville, 171
Tausendteufel, 5
Tennyson, 39
Thésée, 189
Tilley, Arthur, 112, 113n.
Tillyard, E. M. W., 17
Titian, 148
Touraine, 111
Toynbee, Arnold, 18, 72
Turpin, 25

Universities Quarterly, xiin., 77n.
URSS, 179
Uruguay, 133
Uzès, 180

Valéry, 72, 103
Vaugelas, 102
Vendôme, 111
Venice, 175
Verdurin, 170, 171, 172
Verdurin, Mme, 170
Verhaeren, Emile, 138 and n., 139, 140, 141
Verlaine, 92, 119, 146–60
Victoria, 4
Vigny, Alfred de, 27, 67
Vinaver, Eugène, xvi n., 89, 94, 95, 99, 158n.
Vinteuil, 171, 174
Virgil, 127
Vogue, La, 134, 138, 157
Voltaire, 42n., 96

Wagner, Richard, 129–30, 145
Wain, John, 190
Wales, xiii.
Wales, University of, 14n.
Walter, André, 182
Waterloo, 5
Watteau, Antoine, 138, 147, 148
West, Rebecca, 131
Whitman, 103, 138
Whitworth Gallery, The, 169n.
Wilson, Colin, 190
Wordsworth, 169, 173, 174
Wyndham, George, 108 and n., 111

Zola, 162